Work on

a Rotten

Day

Work on a Rotten Day

ASTROLOGICAL ADVICE
FOR OUTWITTING
CONNIVING COWORKERS,
SLACKER STAFF,
AND THE BOSS FROM HELL

Hazel Dixon-Cooper

gpp®
life

Guilford, Connecticut
An imprint of Globe Pequot Press

GPP Life is an imprint of Globe Pequot Press.

Text and PopOut designed by Sheryl P. Kober

Library of Congress Cataloging-in-Publication Data is available on file.

ISBN 978-0-7627-5089-4

Printed in China

10 9 8 7 6 5 4 3 2 1

For the Fridays—
Bonnie Hearn Hill, the resourceful Gemini;
Sheree Petree, the determined Scorpio;
Christopher Allen Poe, the hard-driving Aries;
Dr. Dennis Lewis, the innovative Aquarius—
with love and gratitude

Contents

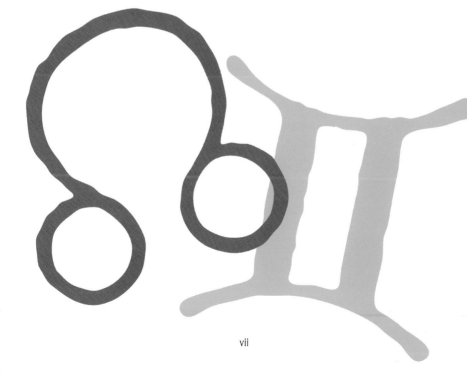

Make the Zodiac Work for You

I do not like work, even when someone else does it.

—Samuel Clemens (November 30)

Work sucks.

Admit it. If it weren't for the paycheck, most of us wouldn't drag ourselves out of bed each morning. Few of us wake up eager to rush out the door and embrace the latest onslaught of on-the-job crises. Yet we all have the power to not only survive any job, and in any job market, but to make *it* work for *us* while we pursue our perfect career.

You're about to learn the real secret of getting ahead. By developing the personal clout of your Sun sign, you can learn to focus your strengths, understand why you shoot yourself in the foot, and prevent that kind of self-sabotage. Knowing the basic traits of other zodiac signs will help you to use their faults to your advantage. You may have read every how-to book on the market or attended every leadership training program around. Still, until you learn what makes your boss, coworkers, staff, and yourself tick—on a soul level—you'll miss the essential ingredient that gives you a competitive edge.

Maybe you're a go-getter who's not afraid of responsibility. You argue for what you think is right, and you're constantly on the lookout for ways to improve. Or you're diligent and dedicated. You never miss work, even when you're sick, and are the one person the boss counts on to put in last-minute overtime. Perhaps you're a manager who's fair minded, friendly, and more coach than CEO. So why aren't you getting either the kudos or respect that you deserve? Or worse, you aren't moving up the career ladder? Ever stop to think that your loyalty might make you the office doormat or that your drive to succeed is perceived as ruthless aggression?

Each Sun sign has soul-level behavior patterns that naturally incline us to act, or react, in certain ways. When not used properly, even your most well-intended actions will work against your career success. Whether you're a cubicle captive slogging through a brain-deadening routine, a slave to the boss from hell, or the supervisor of a slacker staff, recognizing the unconscious behaviors of others gives you an advantage. The important key to success is learning how to handle *you*. Do that, and everything will fall into place.

Sir Francis Drake said, "Knowledge is power." In a nutshell, what he meant was that understanding something gives you control. Understand yourself, and you develop control of your actions and reactions. Understand why you shouldn't confront a Fire sign, when to argue with an Air sign, what motivates an Earth sign, and how to avoid dramas with a Water sign, and you'll take control of your work environment.

It's time to stop feeling like the proverbial rodent trapped on the hamster wheel to nowhere. Start using the influence of the zodiac to arm yourself with a knowledge that will help you to impress your boss, inspire your staff, outsmart a rival, win the loyalty of your coworkers, and jump on the fast track to success.

ASTROLOGY BASICS

Just as each of us might have recognizable family traits, habits, or looks, we are also distinct individuals. You might have inherited your grandfather's temper or the color of your mother's hair. Your siblings could be shorter or taller. Everyone has a different blend of genetic characteristics.

Astrology is the same. No two birth charts are precisely alike, even for multiple-birth babies. A natal chart is based upon the exact placement of the planets and houses of a horoscope at the moment of birth. It's calculated on the date (mm/dd/yy), time, and place of birth. An interpretation of the natal horoscope is an in-depth study that reveals your strengths, weaknesses, talents, and challenges.

Sun sign astrology is a general overview of each zodiac sign. While every Airy Libra may not be shallow or vain, you can bet that one will seldom make snap decisions, even with Fire in his or her chart. Or every Gemini might not persistently bite off more than he or she can chew but will probably have a wide and varied circle of friends and acquaintances.

In astrology, there are four *elements*—*Fire, Earth, Air,* and *Water;* three *qualities*—*Cardinal, Fixed,* and *Mutable;* and two *dualities*—*Masculine* and *Feminine.* Each sign is a combination of one element, one quality, and one duality. This unique blend modifies the Sun sign, which helps to explain the differences between people with the same sign. Each sign is *"ruled"* by one of the nine planets in our solar system, adding another layer to the Sun sign character.

The Elements: Fire, Earth, Air, and Water
Fire signs are Aries, Leo, and Sagittarius.

- Terms associated with Fire signs are *active, confident, opinionated,* and, sometimes, *arrogant.*
- At work, their enthusiastic drive can be wasted stuck in a routine job. This often leads to a frustrated goof-off who causes trouble just to keep things interesting. They work hard, but without strong leadership, they'll eventually try to take over.

Earth signs are Taurus, Virgo, and Capricorn.

- Descriptions of Earth signs include *habitual, stable, calm,* and, occasionally, *rigid.*

- Professionally, these folks thrive on structure. Without focus, though, an Earth sign's strength of purpose can skew into either a routine-addicted plodder or an overbearing fault finder who spends more time complaining about problems than seeking solutions.

Air signs are Gemini, Libra, and Aquarius.
- Key words for Air signs are *informative, resourceful,* and *analytical.* Easily *distracted* is one of their negative traits.
- Career or otherwise, these people are the communicators. Isolate them, and their talent for brainstorming ideas morphs into a flair for wasting time on personal business and meaningless gossip.

Water signs are Cancer, Scorpio, and Pisces.
- While Water signs are *creative, dutiful,* and *insightful, manipulative* is another description that is also attributed them.
- On or off the job, Water sign people take everything personally. They need to feel valued, or they simply emotionally check out.

The Qualities: Cardinal (forceful), Fixed (stable), and Mutable (adaptable)

Aries, Cancer, Libra, and Capricorn are the Cardinal signs.
- Key words associated with Cardinal signs are *dominant* and *influential,* as well as *overbearing* and *authoritarian.* They *originate* change and *provoke* conflict.
- These are the colleagues who want to do things their way despite appearing to go along with the consensus. They tend to ignore the rules, try to take the lead whether they're qualified or not, and get confrontational when challenged.

Taurus, Leo, Scorpio, and Aquarius are the Fixed signs.

- Core traits of Fixed signs are *loyal* and *routine loving, opinionated,* and *inflexible.* They *resist* change and can *resent* authority.
- They subscribe to the "if it ain't broke, don't fix it" method, with one caveat—unless the idea to change is theirs. They're difficult to persuade, independent, and prefer to move at their own pace.

Gemini, Virgo, Sagittarius, and Pisces are the Mutable signs.

- Descriptions of Mutable people include *multitasking, flexible,* and *variety loving.* They *initiate* ideas and *rationalize* to prove a point.
- Without a specific plan, this easily distracted group loses focus. They are team players and negotiators. They also can procrastinate or scatter their energies and get little or nothing accomplished.

The Dualities: Masculine (assertive) and Feminine (receptive)

Aries, Gemini, Leo, Libra, Sagittarius, and Aquarius (Fire and Air) are the Masculine signs.

- Words associated with these individuals are *proactive, sociable,* and *confident.* Their flip side is *arrogant, vain,* and *pushy.*
- They're willing to take risks, like change, and seek excitement. They also tend to overreact, leap without looking, and verbally hammer others in order to get their way.

Taurus, Cancer, Virgo, Scorpio, Capricorn, and Pisces (Earth and Water) are the Feminine signs.

- Traits linked to these men and women include *reactive, perceptive,* and *committed.* Plus *passive, reserved,* and *deliberate.*
- These people are insightful, reliable, and hardworking. They are also inclined to stage-manage others from behind the scenes, maneuver for control, and avoid even positive confrontation.

Planetary Rulers

- Mars, the planet of competition, courage, and energy, rules Aries.
- Venus, the planet of love and beauty, rules both Taurus and Libra. Taurus has her traits of control, geniality, and love of material things. Libra has her traits of assistance, courtesy, and lenience.
- Mercury, the planet of communication, rules both Gemini and Virgo. Gemini has his traits of eloquence, shrewdness, and versatility. Virgo has his traits of criticism, skill, and unhurriedness.
- The emotional, inconsistent, security-craving Moon rules Cancer.
- The proud, authoritarian, center-of-everything Sun rules Leo.
- Pluto, the planet of defiance, self-control, and scrutiny, rules Scorpio.
- Jupiter, the planet of diversion, drive, and honesty, rules Sagittarius.
- Saturn, the planet of ambition, economy, and tradition rules Capricorn.
- Uranus, the planet of analysis, innovation, and radicalism, rules Aquarius.

- Neptune, the planet of affability, deception, and vision, rules Pisces.

As you can see from the above variables, there's a lot you can learn about a person from just his or her Sun sign.

Let's compare a couple of examples: Taurus is Fixed Feminine Earth. These natives are *stable* (Earth), *receptive* (Feminine) and *inflexible* (Fixed). Taurus is ruled by Venus, which gives them a need for security and comfort. Virgo is also *stable* (Earth) and *receptive* (Feminine). The difference is that Virgos are Mutable and ruled by Mercury, which makes them more *flexible* and *communicative*.

Now that you have the basics, when you put it all together, you'll have an edge on knowing how to handle a tough boss, inspire a listless employee, and outsmart a backstabbing coworker.

Best of all, you'll learn how to avoid your personal pitfalls, boost your natural gifts, and step out of your own way to success.

CHAPTER ONE

Digging Deeper

It's never too late to be what you might have been.

GEORGE ELIOT (NOVEMBER 22*)

*ON ELIOT'S DATE OF BIRTH (NOVEMBER 22, 1819), THE SUN WAS IN
THE SIGN OF SCORPIO, NOT SAGITTARIUS AS IS COMMON TODAY.

Are you a job jumper or a workaholic, disorganized and distracted, or a control freak who can't delegate a pizza run for lunch? Do you believe the end justifies the means or feel that you're always misunderstood?

Many factors affect your overall job aptitude and attitude. However, in addition to your Sun sign, there are two other significant astrological influences on your job or career: (1) the Sun signs that rule the Sixth and Tenth Houses of your chart (this can be any sign, not only your personal Sun sign) and (2) whether any planets are located in either, or both, of these houses.

An astrology chart is a twelve-sectioned pie chart. Each section represents one area of life and is ruled by one of the twelve Sun signs. Each Sun sign has a specific energy it brings to the house in which it's located. In this book, I'm going to teach you some basics about how that energy transforms the life area represented by the Sixth and Tenth Houses.

The starting point of every natal (birth) astrology chart is the First House. The sign that rules the First House is commonly called your Rising sign, or what astrologers call the Ascendant. The Sun sign that falls here is based on your birth data of date (mm/dd/yy), time, and place, and determines the placement of every other sign within the houses on your personal birth chart wheel. Think of it as the code key that makes all the pieces click into place, sort of like the tumblers on a combination lock. If you don't have a personal astrology chart, it's easy to get one. Do an Internet search for "free astrology chart." Most astrology sites produce a chart wheel, plus a user-friendly list of where your planets are and what your Rising sign is.

Every chart is a picture of intersecting lines and strange-looking symbols that can look complicated and foreign. Don't worry. Right now, all you need to know is the sign that rules the Sixth and Tenth Houses, and whether any planets are located there. For example, let's say our subject has a Pisces Sun and her Rising sign is Scorpio. With Scorpio in the First House, and counting counterclockwise, the zodiac sign ruling the Sixth House would be Aries[1], and the influence is from Mars. In the Tenth,

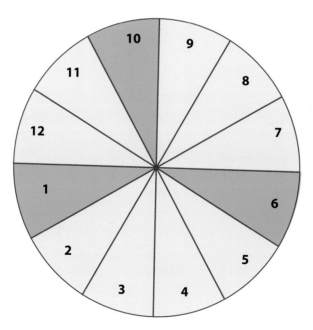

---

[1] Scorpio, Sagittarius, Capricorn, Aquarius, Pisces, *Aries*

Leo[2], with the Sun's influence. This means that the area of life represented by the house takes on the traits of the sign that rules it. Add a planet, and it deepens, or *activates,* the traits of that house with its energy and is a strong influence that contributes to your on-the-job achievements and conflicts.

Translation? If the planet Mars was in our example's Sixth House, it would make non-confrontational Pisces much more inclined to be outspoken and competitive at work. Or if Jupiter happened to land in her Tenth House, this Fish would be more apt to swim with the sharks to seek public recognition, and most likely find it.

What if your Sixth or Tenth House is ruled by one of the other signs, but the planet Mars is located there? Read the sections on both the sign that rules and the planet that occupies the house. For example, say that our subject had Scorpio as the ruling sign in her Sixth House. If the planet Mars is there, too, then read the section on Pluto/Scorpio and the section on Mars/Aries.

What if you want to know more about your boss and don't have her Rising sign? Well, there's a simple way to get a sneak preview of the general behind-the-scenes activity called the *Solar Chart Method.* The good news is that you don't even need a chart for this technique. If you know the person's Sun sign, simply use that as the First House sign and count counterclockwise through the signs to the Sixth or Tenth House.

For example, if the person is a Pisces Sun, the ruling sign in the Sixth House is Leo, and in the Tenth, Capricorn. (Look at the Table of Contents in this book to see the correct order of the Sun signs.) While very general because it applies to every person with that Sun sign, it does provide clues to his or her work ethic and career approach.

The *Solar Chart Method* is what we astrologers use to write the general horoscopes that appear in magazines and newspapers.

---

[2] Scorpio, Sagittarius, Capricorn, Aquarius, Pisces, Aries, Taurus, Gemini, Cancer, *Leo*

Astro Tip

Next time you read the *Cosmo Astrologer* (or any general horoscope), read your Rising sign as well as your Sun sign for a more personalized prediction.

Okay, now you're armed with either your own astro info or the Sun sign of the person you want to check up on. The next sections describe these influences and help you to uncover even more secrets you can use to get a jump on the competition.

THE SIXTH HOUSE

There are two separate parts of the Sixth House, *health* and *work*. Since we know that work-related stressors can affect our health, it's important to see how these areas blend.

First, think of the Sixth House as representing an everyday job. This is the work you do for someone else (or that someone else does for you) or services you provide to others, how you approach or delegate that work, and some professions you might be good at or be drawn to. Do you rebel at being bossed? Are you more comfortable working on a team? Is your self-esteem wrapped up in your work?

Second, notice how both the ruling sign and any planets that land there might affect your emotional and physical health in relation to your work.

Planets and Signs through the Sixth House
Moon / Cancer

People with the Moon in the Sixth House are emotionally tied to their jobs. Consciously or not, colleagues are often treated as family versus professionally. Conflicts and everyday pressures that might simply annoy any other sign can literally make you sick.

Strengths:
- Compassionate work with the public
- Successful at home-based businesses
- Good at behind-the-scenes support
- Generous with encouragement

Challenges:
- Gets sick when the pressure's on
- Uses subterfuge instead of fighting fair
- Has high turnover of employees due to inconsistent leadership
- Changes jobs frequently due to conflicts

Advice:

Those with the Moon in the Sixth House or with Cancer as the ruling sign should strive for objectivity. Beware of getting emotionally involved in the lives of coworkers. Cancer is associated with the breasts and female reproductive organs. In the Sixth House it can cause obsessive worry over work or tension with colleagues, which can lead to vague physical illnesses and excessive time off—plus, a permanent-PMS personality that results in constant conflict.

Avoid eating lunch at your desk, don't get caught up in grapevine gossip, and learn to recognize your moods so that you understand the world isn't really out to get you.

If you work with Sixth House Moon children, always approach them in a calm manner to earn their trust.

Sun / Leo

Work and health are of near-equal importance with the Sun in the Sixth House. Here, the ego is wrapped up with ambition, drive, and physical fitness. You appreciate recognition of your efforts and frequent head pats.

Strengths:
- Takes pride in work
- Is dedicated
- Does well in the healing professions
- Has a common-sense approach to maintaining health

Challenges:
- Bitches incessantly about job and coworkers
- Spends more time avoiding work than doing it
- Refuses to do tasks that he or she considers boring or beneath him/her
- Either refuses to admit it when sick or is obsessed with health and appearance

Advice:

Anyone with his or her Sun in the Sixth House or with Leo as the ruling sign should be particularly aware of how stress relates to health issues. Leo rules the heart and back, so these natives benefit from proper ergonomics, cardiovascular exercise, and a heart-healthy diet.

Be aware of ego trips and acting as if you're better than your colleagues.

If you work with a Sixth House Sun person, a little ego stroking goes a long way toward earning his or her cooperation.

Mercury / Gemini or Virgo

As Mercury rules both Gemini and Virgo, it reflects traits of both when it lands in the Sixth House. If Gemini is the ruling sign, communications or writing might be a skill. If Virgo, you might be interested in nutrition, hygiene, or small animals.

No matter what the ruling sign might be, networking is one of your strengths, but dealing with all those people can also drive you nuts.

Strengths:

- Learns fast
- Good at multitasking
- Likes to keep busy
- Does well in teaching, research, or physical fitness occupations

Challenges:

- Refuses to delegate even if overwhelmed with work
- Gets preoccupied with so many details that little is accomplished
- Talks too much
- Memo-happy

Advice:

Mercury in the Sixth House brings a variety of work-health issues. Gemini rules the lungs, wrists, hands, shoulders, and nervous system. Virgo rules the digestive tract and also significantly affects the nervous system. Stressors include chronic irritability, anxiety, and a tendency to be high-strung. You need daily time in the fresh air and can benefit from meditation, soothing background music, and a PDA.

Communication is one of your strengths, but be aware that you don't hog the conversation or ignore input from your coworkers.

A couple of ways to win over Sixth House Mercury colleagues would be to help them research a project or catch up on their bottomless stack of paperwork.

Venus / Taurus or Libra

Venus also rules two signs, Taurus and Libra, and reflects the traits of both signs when it's parked in the Sixth House. If Taurus is the ruling sign, then money and stability is important. With Libra, it's cooperation and harmony.

Whichever sign of the zodiac is in charge, your overall health is boosted with Venus here—as long as you're consistent in following a healthy diet and regular exercise.

You must like what you do to succeed, can be the company peace-maker, and could end up marrying your boss, a coworker, or someone you meet through your job.

Strengths:

- Has talent for counseling, artistic, and law-related professions
- Is well liked by clients, colleagues, and the boss
- Enjoys working with others
- Cooperates and makes valuable contributions to team projects

Challenges:

- Has a tit-for-tat mentality
- Terminally critical and nitpicky about everything from a coworker's abilities to the temperature
- Wastes time on personal tasks
- Overindulges both physically and emotionally

Advice:

Libra controls the kidneys and lower back. Taurus controls the throat and appetite. Venus is the planet of self-indulgence, so it's very important that you stick to the *all-things-in-moderation* rule. This especially applies to fattening food and any kind of sweets. You can benefit from low-impact exercise, and you should beware of stuffing your face due to stress.

You'll usually work better with a partner or a team than alone, and you'll feel better when you add personal touches that make your work area feel homey.

Win a Venus colleague's allegiance with public praise, a show of camaraderie, and a plate of his or her favorite cookies.

Mars/Aries

Hot-tempered, easily bored Mars adds energy and assertiveness to the way you approach both your work and your health. Accidents can happen because you're always in a rush, and there's a danger that you could get caught hooking up with a coworker.

You want to be where the action is and aren't afraid to tackle any project or fight for what you want.

Strengths:

- Seeks challenging tasks and projects
- Likes to stay busy
- Chooses professions that involve some emotional, financial, or physical risk
- Dedicates him- or herself to the company

Challenges:

- Argues over *everything*
- Thinks he or she is above the rules
- Piles so much work on subordinates that they either snap or strike
- Looks to others for motivation

Advice:

Mars or Aries in the Sixth House rules the head and face. Work-related stress can cause tension headaches and high blood pressure, not to mention the wrinkles you'll get from permanently scowling at everyone. High-energy workouts will help to keep you in top physical and mental shape.

You don't mind burning the midnight oil or helping with menial tasks to get the job done. But you need balance in your life to keep from burning out.

Win the loyalty of Mars-fueled associates by telling them that you can't get along without them.

Jupiter / Sagittarius

Freedom-loving Jupiter in the Sixth House has a need for on-the-job independence and a natural aversion to being supervised. This is another indicator of strong physical health. As Jupiter is *the* planet of excess, food obsessions and extreme behaviors are also a part of the package with this placement and can threaten your well-being. However, Jupiter here also adds luck to your working life—you're rarely without a job or an opportunity to prosper.

You like a fast-paced career and are usually optimistic, no matter how overloaded you are.

Strengths:

- Works well with the public and in highly visible areas
- Handles high-volume workloads
- Has natural ability for publishing, travel, and family-owned businesses
- Likes people and has a calming effect when faced with crises

Challenges:

- Wastes time by being chronically disorganized
- Pigs out under stress
- Ignores boss's priorities in favor of his or her own
- Tends to exaggerate his or her importance

Advice:

Jupiter or Sagittarius in the Sixth House rules the hips and thighs. Make sure not to sit for long periods of time without getting up to stretch or walk for a few minutes. Plus, you'll avoid the nonstop snacking at your desk that contributes to a two-axe-handle-wide ass. Energy levels are boundless, and you're usually highly active.

There are few people who can outwork you or who are as willing to help others succeed, but beware of people who'd take advantage of you.

Make friends with Jupiter-ruled teammates by inviting them to lunch and letting them talk about themselves.

Saturn / Capricorn

A Sixth House Saturn indicates that you're a hard worker with a tendency to become a workaholic. No goofing off is allowed under stern Saturn, so you must be diligent and committed in order to succeed. Healthwise,

Saturn here can make you susceptible to catching every bug that comes along. Protect yourself by carrying hand sanitizer, drinking lots of water, and taking extra precautions during the flu and cold seasons.

You tend to worry too much about losing your job and usually do well in long-term positions or professions where you can methodically move up the ladder.

Strengths:
- Sees a project or task through to its completion
- Sticks through tough times and last-minute deadlines
- Has aptitude for professions that require economy, patience, and organizational skills
- Outlasts the competition

Challenges:
- Worries excessively about things that may never happen
- Gets stuck in a rut
- Reacts slowly to change and stresses over it
- Can neglect health, which leads to serious illness

Advice:
There's no free ride when Saturn or Capricorn is in the Sixth House. You have to pay your dues before earning success and pay attention to your health to avoid serious issues. Saturn rules the knees, teeth, and bones. Be aware of clenching your jaws under stress. As depression and gloomy thoughts are associated with Saturn, long walks in the fresh air are good for your emotional as well as physical health.

Setting manageable goals helps you to achieve your dream. Be sure to reward yourself as you accomplish each step to stay upbeat and motivated.

Saturn-ruled people appreciate comrades who are cheerful. Get on their A-list by avoiding doom-and-gloom gossip and offering to assist them when they're jamming.

Uranus / Aquarius

Sudden opportunities or unexpected setbacks can happen with a Sixth House Uranus. You need a challenge and are apt to abruptly quit or transfer if your job becomes boring. Routine is definitely not your cup of tea, and being your own boss might be your ideal situation. Health issues can pop up suddenly or come at highly inconvenient times.

Your intuition can help you to spot the next fad or trend, and you usually prefer to work alone.

Strengths:

- Likes to be on the cutting edge of the latest techniques and technology
- Enjoys being the guinea pig for new systems and processes
- Shifts easily between projects
- Benefits from self-employment, and fund-raising, teaching, or innovative occupations

Challenges:

- Skips the details, which causes errors and sloppy work
- Hates routine and isn't a team player
- Thinks that he or she always has a better way and often insists on doing it that way
- Quits without notice

Advice:

When Uranus or Aquarius rules the Sixth House, you're highly attuned to your surroundings. This can make you jittery and prone to internalizing stress, which results in sickness. It's wise for you not to eat when you're upset, angry, or stressed out at work. Keep calm with meditation, getting out of the office at lunch, and yoga.

Don't be too eager to job-jump, or employers eventually won't risk hiring you. Instead, ask for challenging assignments and attend seminars and workshops. You'll stay motivated and one step ahead of the pack.

Earn Uranus-ruled associates' admiration by discussing a new development or idea and asking them for their opinion.

Neptune / Pisces

Illusion-inducing Neptune in the Sixth House can result in unrealistic ideas about your job. You tend to be idealistic and avoid looking at things as they are, which can keep you from recognizing your on-the-job enemies until it's too late. This impractical trait can affect your attitude toward your health, too. You also tend to procrastinate on healthy changes and can absorb the negative vibes of others.

You have a strong intuitive sense about your work and colleagues. Learn to listen to and trust your own judgment.

Strengths:
- Can be successful at holistic medicine, psychology, and photography
- Works well behind the scenes or where secrets and confidentiality must be maintained
- Shows new colleagues the ropes
- Can work in one-man areas or in out-of-the-way places

Challenges:
- Gets involved in deceptive or secret alliances at work
- Blames mistakes on coworkers
- Has an unreal perception of what is expected of them
- Gets confused about job duties and responsibilities

Advice:
When Neptune or Pisces rules the Sixth House, misunderstandings, wrong perceptions, and dubious work habits are always a danger. So are health issues due to hypochondria, drug allergies, and a lack of self-discipline. Stay away from the office whiner, because your sensitive nature can make you receptive to "catching" their negative attitude.

Get your job duties in writing and refer to them often to stay on track. Using your natural intuition to develop creative problem-solving skills will earn you kudos and boost your self-confidence.

Thoughtful acts, such as reminding them of an upcoming appointment or sharing your meeting notes, earns you bonus points with Neptune-ruled colleagues.

Sneaky Ways to Suss out Someone's Sun Sign when You Don't Want to Ask

- Make friends with a human resources staffer and promise to give her the scoop on *her* boss and coworkers
- Use your department or company newsletter's list of monthly birthdays
- Start your own monthly birthday e-mail notice for your area

Pluto / Scorpio

Having total control over your daily routine is important with Pluto in your Sixth House. You like to be left alone to do your work and hate interruptions of any kind, especially unannounced coworkers who drop in to chat. There's a karmic aspect to having a Sixth House Pluto or Scorpio as the ruling sign in that you have a responsibility to be of service to others. You can rebound from illness with amazing speed.

Your powers of concentration are stellar, and you have a talent for reorganizing priorities, projects, and even your work environment in a much more efficient way.

Strengths:

- Has excellent powers of concentration and stamina
- Excels at investigative, research, legal, and medical professions
- Supports superiors and colleagues
- Uses insight and shrewd maneuvering to outwit the competition

Challenges:
- Can be a total control freak
- Pushes boundaries with no intention of compromise
- Has an *"I'll get you for that"* mentality
- Is out for his- or herself and to hell with the rest of the world

Advice:

Pluto or Scorpio in the Sixth House adds an obsessive edge to the way you feel about your job. Your health is often linked to your emotional state, so try to consciously let go of anger and resentment. Music has an especially healing affect on you. If it's allowed, consider keeping a radio tuned to your favorite jazz or soothing-sounds station on your desk.

Beware of wanting so much control over your work that you fail to take good advice. You can save yourself lots of time and trouble by listening to and learning from your coworkers. Plus, revenge may be sweet, but it won't pay the rent.

It takes time to win over these coworkers. To prove that you're trustworthy, keep their secrets, respect their privacy, and ask their advice about a career move.

THE TENTH HOUSE

The Tenth House of your natal chart represents your career potential (versus a mundane job), long-range goals, and the achievements or influence of your father or his side of your family. Your desire for public recognition, your reputation, fame (or infamy), and the authority figures who might help or hinder you are here. As well as how you could shoot yourself in the foot.

The planet and/or sign that rules your Tenth House reveals the type of careers you might have a natural interest in or talent for (a few are listed at the end of each chapter), how you approach your career, and what you'd be willing to do or not do to achieve it.

Planets and Signs through the Tenth House
Moon / Cancer

Public admiration or to lead a public life is a dream for a Tenth House Moon. Whether you'll be rich and famous is never certain, but if you work at it, you can achieve some type of public recognition. You get emotional satisfaction from climbing a career ladder or seeing a long-term goal become a reality.

Because the Moon rules family-oriented Cancer, someone in your family might also achieve fame—either as a star or an outlaw. It also can create many ups and downs along your career path due to its changeable nature.

Potential:
- Inspirational leader
- Financial planner
- Caterer, restaurateur, or bakery owner
- Real estate broker or interior designer
- Family business or same career of either parent
- Travel agent or travel industry

Dangers:
- Keeping up appearances at the cost of your private life
- Being unable to handle day-to-day pressures or make quick decisions
- Giving up before you give yourself a chance to succeed

Advice:
A Tenth House Moon can cause inconsistent support from others, create unnecessary drama, and generate confusion. Always make yourself clear or hire a public relations agent to avoid misunderstandings that can lead to your discredit or public scandal. Overcome delays and minor setbacks by mapping out your plan before you start. Influential women can provide insight and guidance.

Sun / Leo

If you're a Tenth House Sun, it's highly unlikely that you're the type to sit and watch the world go by, even if you're a shy Pisces or reclusive Scorpio. With the Sun or Leo here, you can feel compelled to make your mark on the world, whether you're a well-respected public servant or a power-hungry politician.

This is a great position for potential success. It's a sign of good character, a steady climb up the career ladder, and for getting a hand up from power players who are impressed by your talents.

Your father might play an important role in your desire to achieve success, either by his example and support, or because you're out to prove that you can do better than he did.

Potential:

- Actor
- Doctor, nurse, or other healing profession
- Business or professional leader
- Speculator
- Boss or supervisor
- Politician or government official

Dangers:

- Letting your pride prevent you from admitting mistakes
- Getting arrogant and forgetting that those who helped build you up can also help to bring you down
- Being greedy. Remember to share the wealth, morally, spiritually, and financially.

Advice:

Just as the real Sun lights up the sky, Tenth House Suns want to light up the world, or at least their corner of it. While this is one of the lucky placements to have in your natal chart, it doesn't guarantee success. You have to do your part by pursuing your career honestly and keeping your ego under control.

When the conquering heroes of ancient Rome returned home in all their glory to the cheers of the crowds, a servant rode with them through the streets to remind them that *all fame is fleeting*. Make this your mantra to help keep you grounded.

Mercury / Gemini or Virgo

Everything from writing letters to writing the next great American novel can appeal to a Tenth House Mercury. You achieve success through innovative ideas and a resourceful character. You could work from behind the scenes to propel other people into the spotlight through teaching or as a speech writer.

You might have either an exceptionally easy or an exceptionally difficult time communicating with your father, or you could have accompanied him on lots of short trips.

Mercury rules both Gemini and Virgo. If Gemini, you could have dual careers (businesswoman by day, writer by night). In Virgo, you might be interested in journalism and travel.

Whichever zodiac sign rules the Tenth House, Mercury here adds adaptability and a flair for communicating.

Potential:

- Architect
- Salesperson working on commission
- Publisher, editor, or novelist
- Reporter or foreign correspondent
- Teacher, speech therapist, or translator
- Handyman

Dangers:

- Restlessness that prevents you from settling on one career
- Lying that comes back to bite you and ruin your reputation
- Impulsive behaviors that lead you to trust the wrong people

Advice:

A Tenth House Mercury likes to match wits with other people. Just be sure that you don't open your mouth at the wrong time or get smart with the wrong person.

It's better if you get established in one career before trying to pursue a second one. Otherwise, you could scatter your energies and fail at both. Networking can pay off big time for you.

Venus / Taurus or Libra

Popularity, charm, talent, and good looks belong to Tenth House Venus people. While you might not have all four, it's almost certain that you are blessed with one or two of these fortunate traits. You're usually popular, and you might know or be related to one of the rich and famous.

Whether you're the best voice in the choir or destined to be the next star on Broadway, Venus here is a good sign of performing talent as well as other artistic skills. You might have inherited your looks or talent from one of your parents.

Venus rules both Taurus and Libra. If Libra happens to be in your Tenth House, you might give fabulous parties and lead an active social life. If Taurus rules, you might be interested in making furniture or collecting or selling fine art.

Potential:

- Entertainment and the arts
- Jewelry or fashion design
- Plastic surgeon or beauty-related professions
- Diplomat
- Horticulture-related occupations or florist
- Interior decorator, housekeeping services

Dangers:

- Believing your own press and becoming a selfish drama queen or king

- Using others to get what you want
- Being too lazy to develop your potential

Advice:

Virtually every Tenth House Venus has some kind of talent or ability to earn a good, if not, spectacular, living. This placement gives you a natural edge over the competition. The risk is in thinking that the world will fall at your feet. It might, but unless you work at perfecting your craft, you could end up just another cute lounge lizard wowing the audience on karaoke night.

Working in any industry associated with providing products or services to women can boost your earning power.

Mars / Aries

A Tenth House Mars bestows a colossal will to make something of yourself. The caveat is that, unless you can rein in your aggression, you could also become a colossal jerk whom no one wants to be around. This placement is a dual-edged sword because your great qualities of determination, drive, and independence can easily turn into blind ambition.

You may work behind the scenes, but you want public recognition of your efforts and have no trouble singing your own praises to get noticed. You might have had more than the average number of fights with your parents or had a domineering father, which gives you an *"I'll show them"* mindset. This attitude could make you rebel against any kind of authority.

Potential:

- Business owner
- Athlete
- Carpenter, builder, or engineer
- Police officer or firefighter, or any occupation that requires courage
- Surgeon
- CEO or other high-level business executive

Dangers:
- Being self-centered and having a single-mindedness about your career could mean you end up alone
- Having a ruthless edge that creates trouble and enemies
- Being domineering

Advice:
Mars or Aries in the Tenth House gives you equal amounts of chutzpah and ruthlessness. Channeling this natural aggression into physical exercise or fighting for the underdogs of life goes a long way to helping take the edge off so that you're less hotheaded and demanding.

Once you learn to treat people with the same respect you demand from them, almost nothing can stop your climb to the top.

Jupiter / Sagittarius

Everything about Jupiter is big, and in the Tenth House he can create big dreams. You can get lucky breaks that put you on the fast track to success or meet influential people who give you a hand up. Your father or mother might have been generous either with money or advice and encouragement, or all three.

You like people and want to share your wisdom or expertise on a large scale. This placement is another indicator of success in the entertainment or political fields, or other public arena.

Potential:
- Religious calling or philosopher
- Goodwill ambassador
- Professor or education executive
- Judge, lawyer, city councilperson, or other political office
- Sports or entertainment promoter
- Welfare or social worker

Dangers:
- Behaving dishonestly in such a way that can land you in the midst of a lawsuit or in jail
- Overextending your physical, mental, or financial resources
- Exhibiting poor judgment of people or in business dealings

Advice:

While Jupiter/Sagittarius usually brings some sort of good fortune, you could also spend your money faster than you earn it. You could fall for every get-rich-quick scheme around or have a con artist's love of pulling a fast one now and then.

Tenth House Jupiter needs an education to flourish. It might not be college. Seminars, workshops, hands-on-training, or an apprenticeship will all help you learn how to focus your considerable power and come out a winner.

Saturn / Capricorn

Saturn is the natural ruler of the Tenth House, which means that few people will have stronger career aims than you. You're persistent, steady, and rarely give up on a goal. But even on his home turf, Saturn never hands anything to anyone on a silver platter. You'll have to work hard, but you also have Saturn's power to push you forward.

This is the classic father-figure placement; you might have had a domineering father, or you could have had to assume a father- or parent-like responsibility for your family at a young age.

Success can come at a price for you, but you should have the will, brains, and fortitude to overcome almost any adversity and climb to the top.

Potential:
- Manager or other positions that require good organizational skills
- Geologist
- Science, cardiology, or other professions where meticulous skill and patience are needed

- Gardener or farmer
- Contractor
- Leather crafting or design

Dangers:

- Losing it all by spreading yourself too thin trying to have it all
- Worrying too much about what others think
- Abusing your power or position over others, which earns you a karmic kick in the butt and leaves you at the bottom of the heap

Advice:

Tenth House Saturn/Capricorn adds a serious edge to your personality and sometimes can make you so determined to succeed that you forget to live. You might also have an overworked sense of guilt that equates having fun with wasting time.

Set aside a rainy-day fund for the inevitable ups and downs that happen. Learn to lighten up with regular time-outs for recreation—movies, bowling, dinner with your most cheerful friends.

Uranus / Aquarius

With Uranus, life is full of surprises, including sudden changes in your career path. Either you decide to head in an entirely new direction or some unexpected event causes an upheaval. You're another soul who could walk two career paths simultaneously: one that's considered unconventional or eccentric, and the other a traditional type.

This placement indicates that your father or his family might have had an unusual career or were nonconformists in some way. There might have been a sudden separation from him or your family. Maybe you left home at an early age to investigate the world.

You're fortunate in that you should be able to make a living in a nontraditional way if you choose.

Potential:

- Psychologist, metaphysical professional, hypnotist
- Astrologer or other New Age practitioner
- Musician, abstract artist, antiquities or oddities dealer
- Computer technology professional, electrical engineer, or a position in other technologies
- Humanitarian
- Mechanic or machinist

Dangers:

- Having a sarcastic mouth that gets you fired before you have a chance to quit.
- Not paying attention to your intuition. It's usually accurate.
- Being accident-prone on or off the job (especially around machinery, explosives, or electricity).

Advice:

Uranus/Aquarius gives you a healthy curiosity, and much of it's directed toward unusual, hidden, or outlandish things in life. You can be a genuine innovator and inventor. However, making a career out of reading tea leaves or studying the mating habits of tree toads in the Amazon rain forest isn't likely to put much food on the table.

Always keep one foot on the ground while you pursue your higher ideals.

Neptune / Pisces

Mystery, glamour, and inspiration surround a Tenth House Neptune. Careers that reflect any of these traits can put you on top of the world. You might want to take a complex subject and bring it to the masses by demystifying it through plain talk or writing.

You might have received an early inheritance from one of your parents, or they could have been dreamers who encouraged your dreams.

Consciously or unconsciously, you most likely have an uncanny sixth sense that puts you in the right place at the right time or gives you the ability to intuit a colleague's true motives.

Potential:

- Professions in film, theater, photography, music
- Spiritual healer, leader, teacher
- Pharmacist or drug researcher
- "Water" occupations—naval seaman, marine scientist, diver, or marine animal veterinarian
- Caregiver, hospital worker, or nurse

Dangers:

- Dreaming about your dream job instead of pursuing it.
- Not relating well to your boss or other higher-ups. Think before you speak and tune in when listening to others.
- Having hidden enemies. Not watching your own back could lead to losing your reputation. Keep your guard up.

Advice:

Neptune/Pisces in the Tenth House adds a talent for illusion and deception. You can use these traits to get ahead. They can also be used against you by others because you can be gullible and naive. Developing your powerful insight acts like armor against backstabbers and betrayers. Learn to trust your gut.

Stay attuned, but don't get caught up in office politics or your coworkers' personal dramas. Your sensitivity to the vibes around you can be detrimental to both your emotional and physical health.

Pluto / Scorpio

Pluto *is* the shark with whom those who seek power and control try to swim. Pluto in the Tenth House can make you almost pathologically determined to control your own destiny, which can make you resist authority of any kind. But then you lose out on the advice and mentoring that might help your career.

Pluto has the power to transform. You could be successful at helping people to transform their lives physically, psychologically, or spiritually.

Mystery or secrecy might have surrounded your father's profession, or you could have resisted the lessons he or your family tried to teach you.

Potential:

- Psychiatrist
- Detective, crime scene investigator, spy
- Minister
- Confidential assistant
- Auditor, IRS agent, prosecuting attorney
- Mystery writer, jazz musician

Dangers:

- Disrespecting authority and a lack of conscience that leads to abuse of privileges or power
- Trying to manipulate others to do your work while you take the credit
- Being totally selfish and eventually running off all the people who were willing to help you

Advice:

Pluto or Scorpio in your Tenth House has the power to build you up or knock you down. Your inner magnetism attracts influential persons who are willing and able to help your career. But you must learn to control negative urges to lie, cheat, steal, and/or manipulate your way to the top, or you're very likely to end up losing everything.

This is another tough planet that gives you the strength, savvy, and courage to achieve anything you want—as long as you learn that the end does not justify the means.

CHAPTER TWO

Aries
March 21–April 19

Element:	Fire
Quality:	Cardinal
Symbol:	The Ram
Ruler:	Mars
Key word:	Competitive
Work-a-tude:	Just do it!

INSTANT INSIGHTS

You know what? Life is short. Let's go for it.

ZACH BRAFF (APRIL 6)

Aries is Masculine Cardinal Fire, the sign of courage and action. As spontaneous and impulsive as the warrior god Mars that rules it, the first sign of the zodiac is also its number-one risk taker. Astronomers often call Mars "the angry red planet," and astrologers often refer to Aries men and women as hot-tempered human dynamos. Rams are all about impulsively taking action, then sorting out the issues.

As does fiery Leo, Aries thrives on attention. The difference is that Leo wants to bask in the spotlight of adoration, while a Ram won't hesitate to be annoyingly interruptive, loud, boorish, or just plain obnoxious in order to get noticed. An Aries's strongest trait is persistence. It's also the Ram's worst one.

FAMOUS ARIES FIRSTS

- Sandra Day O'Connor, first woman justice of the Supreme Court (March 26)
- Maya Angelou, first Reynolds Professor of American Studies at Wake Forest University (April 4)
- Wilbur Wright, first man to fly and coinventor of the airplane (April 16)

Leo Fire is fixed and usually focused on its immediate surroundings, and the mutable Sagittarius Fire is cheery and welcoming. Aries Fire can rage as hot as a firestorm that consumes everything in its path without either thought or logic. Link this with a Masculine assertiveness, and it translates to a man or woman who is highly excitable, eager to start new ventures, and not afraid to lay everything on the line to succeed.

Aries enthusiasm can ignite in a nanosecond and flare white hot, but it can't sustain itself for the long haul. That's why many Rams start and stop so many businesses, projects, and plans. Don't confuse this with Gemini's superficial interest in a variety of subjects. Gemini loves knowledge for knowledge's sake, and once they have a basic working grasp of their latest interest, they move to the next.

Astrology teaches us Rams are often so preoccupied with themselves and their aspirations that they can't see any point of view but their own. The First House is about the self, which Aries can be full of. It's also the starting point of any project or relationship, and Mars-fueled Rams always start in high gear. They fear nothing. They stop at nothing. Many accomplish nothing. Why? They plow ahead without logic, forethought, or a plan. Similar to the naive ego of a child, Rams assume they will meet zero resistance from the competition.

It's natural for all of the Cardinal signs to assume they can run things. Watery Cancer acts like the head of the family, guiding and controlling.

Earthy Capricorn sets a high standard and expects everyone to follow their example. Airy Libras try to get their way with charisma. They want to be popular. Aries wants to be *first:* first to make the sales quota, first to finish the research project, first to the scene of the crime.

ARIES ON THE JOB

There's a line in the picture where he snarls, "Nobody tells me what to do." That's exactly how I've felt all my life.

MARLON BRANDO (APRIL 3)

Aries are notorious for doing the exact opposite of what you want them to do. Arguing with them will get you nowhere, for they love to fight. Pleading with them earns their scorn, and appealing to their rational side fails because they don't have one. Aries are famous for emotional head butting, just as the literal head bashing of a real ram.

The secret to getting a Ram to do what you want is a twofold process. First, be tough and keep your guard up. You have to outmaneuver, outwit, and sometimes bump heads to keep Aries on track. Second, dispense equal doses of love and discipline. Every Aries, whether an intern fresh out of college or an old pro getting ready to retire, craves affection and approval. Think of a child craving the adoration of his or her parents, and keep this scene in your head around every Aries you know.

Managing a Ram
Dangle Carrots
Whether an athlete or a receptionist, a firefighter or an entrepreneur, high-energy Rams need high-energy work. Stick an Aries secretary in a boring cubicle transcribing dictation eight hours a day, and you'll get a first-rate office gossip with an excessive sick-day count. Put her in a hot spot where

she can train new employees or work independently for a VIP, and she'll shine. Expect your Ram salesman to slog through a monotonous route visiting the same clients month in and month out, and he'll find a way to shoot himself in the foot by slacking off until his sales are in a slump. Add a new hotshot to his route and dangle an incentive (even if it's a plastic plaque that says he's number one), and he'll kick into gear to prove he's still on top.

Without external incentives, the Aries lack of follow-through can result in a fast-talking salesman who rarely closes a deal or a woman who starts her own business but fails because she hates dealing with the behind-the-scenes details of bookkeeping and inventory control.

Keep Them Enthused

Rams bring the same impulsive reactions to their careers as they do to love. They instantly "fall in love" with the new job. They easily make friends and impress the boss with their go-getter attitude. As with Gemini, once routine kicks in the honeymoon wears off, and that's when conflict starts. Offer new challenges and provide on-the-job learning opportunities to keep them interested.

Money isn't a Ram's prime motivator. Feeling indispensable is. He needs frequent encouragement because your average Aries is usually as eager to please as a kid seeking approval from Mom. Despite a sometimes-brash behavior, an Aries can be as easily wounded as any Water sign. Loyalty means everything. However, it's your loyalty to him first, then his devoted loyalty to you. If a Ram trusts you, he will work his ass off for you, including weekends, holidays, or overtime without complaint.

Imagine a Human Nuclear Reactor

Aries Fire burns furiously and needs strong containment to prevent a full out conflagration. Rams can be innovative, brainstorming whizzes who thrive on outwitting the competition, revamping worn out techniques, and shaking up the status quo. They are not the best team players, as they have trouble sharing credit. As team leaders, they need leadership training and frequent follow-up, for their first instinct is to take command, not to guide others.

From day one, the Ram has to understand who's the boss, because from day one this employee will bend the rules and test your leadership. If "no" becomes "maybe," Aries will instinctively push the boundaries as far as possible. Remember, you're dealing with a person whose Sun sign is ruled by Mars, the god of war, and fighting to be lead *anything* is his second nature.

Aries wants to win, and he wants his team or company to succeed. He's a champ at being the first to help in a crunch, won't hesitate to volunteer to help with a project, and, when properly coached, can teach and inspire others.

An Aries native is as tough as her zodiac symbol, the Ram, and you'll have to be tough to win her loyalty and respect. If you are up to the challenge, you'll be rewarded with a bold, ground-breaking innovator who can help to make your team, department, or business number one.

Surviving Boss Ram
Know What You're Dealing With

A Cancer boss may treat you like a member of the family. A Scorpio boss can be willing to pitch in when you're on overload. The Aries boss, however, expects nothing less than total subordination.

Take-charge Rams bark orders, only believe in teamwork if they control the team, and can have flash-fire tempers. You'll need a thick skin to put up with this human buzz saw for very long.

Benign astrology tells us that Aries bosses are great at fostering self-esteem in their employees and are inspirational leaders. I once knew a female Aries boss who inspired the term *Bitchzilla*. Although she'd only been a VP four years, she went through seven harried personal assistants. The eighth was teetering on the edge, polishing his résumé, when, much to everyone's relief, she decided to leave the company.

Although astrology equates *Cardinal* with *leadership*, in Aries, this combination can be disastrous. A Ram has a driving need to be in charge. It's dangerous to automatically assume that he's a natural leader, however. The Aries independent, take-the-initiative style can produce innovative thinkers and ambitious, goal-oriented managers. The flip side is that Aries as team leaders can become arbitrary aggressors who run their projects or departments like a military unit and expect the same blind obedience as does a drill sergeant.

Be Resilient

So how do you cope, let alone advance, working for a volatile Ram? Most importantly, show no fear. Stay calm when yours is on the attack, and for God's sake, never cry in front of this boss. Even the kindest Aries hates public displays of emotion. Although you might receive a sympathetic hug and a shoulder to lean on, she will mentally file your outburst away as a sign of weakness.

ARIES WORDS TO LIVE BY

"High expectations are the key to everything."
—Sam Walton, founder of Walmart (March 29)

"You can't just sit there and wait for people to give you that golden dream. You've got to get out there and make it happen for yourself."
—Diana Ross (March 26)

Your Aries boss sets the highest expectations for herself and expects nothing less from you. Show the Ram that you are not afraid to suggest new ideas, but keep your presentations short and dynamic, and include a ballpark cost savings or increased production or profits figure. Hint: It's okay to expand your projections a little, as Aries loves big ambitions.

Expect to Work at a Breathless Pace

A Ram isn't afraid to take the initiative and is excellent at coping with internal or external emergencies. However, she despises detail work and is light on follow-up. If you pick up the details or research a competing company she's trying to beat out of a lucrative contract, you'll prove yourself and earn this boss's loyalty.

The greatest thing about an Aries boss is that she absolutely understands and respects drive, motivation, and courage. Don't be afraid to leap into unknown territory with the Ram.

Like the Martian warrior that rules her, working for Boss Ram is a dual-edged sword. On one side, she can be generous to a fault with advances on your salary, liberal vacation time, and extra days off with pay. On the other, it means nothing to her to ask you to cancel your plans for the weekend to help close a big deal. She does it. So should you. Get caught goofing off, and you'll suffer a royal chewing out. However, this is one boss who will also give you many chances to shape up before she actually kicks you out.

Look at it this way: If you can survive reporting to the volatile Ram and manage to earn her respect, working for any other sign in the universe will seem like a breeze.

Coping with an Aries Coworker

An Aries will bounce up, get in your face, and look you directly in the eye as he introduces himself. If you're a shy Taurus or a space-challenged Scorpio, getting used to this feisty, assertive person could take time. He's open, helpful, and willing to show you the ropes. I've never known an Aries who refused to lend a hand when needed.

Be Direct

Your challenge is learning to coexist with perhaps the most self-centered sign in the universe. This doesn't mean this coworker doesn't care whether her constant personal telephone calls and steady stream of visitors might interfere with your concentration. It's that, like Aquarius, the thought never enters her mind to ask you. Further, unless this coworker is so busy that she can't speak, you'll be bombarded with personal tales from her life and pointed questions about yours.

Subtle hints and polite excuses don't work with the Ram. Say that you're too busy to talk and suggest coffee or lunch later. Don't hesitate to ask him to turn down the music or to wait until break time to visit with chums because you have to concentrate on your project. A Ram hates to be ignored, and giving one the silent treatment only makes him more determined to bother you. A Ram appreciates straightforwardness and really is like a kid who's totally unaware that you aren't having as good a time as he.

Keep Your Guard Up

Cutthroat Aries colleagues are formidable opponents. Remember, competing is second nature to this sign. She can be so arrogant that it won't matter whether she's actually qualified to head the prize project—the thought never occurs to a Ram that she won't get it.

Fortunately, your average Ram is about as subtle as a crutch, so you and everyone else will most likely know when you're being rivaled. Beware of a sudden interest in your job or an area of expertise you have that he doesn't. Fight fire with fire and announce your own intention to move up the ladder. The worst type will try to bully you with a comment like, "I'm applying for the promotion," accompanied by an I-dare-you look designed to make you instantly decide to drop out of the race. He won't hesitate to brownnose the boss or any other power player in order to sidestep the process, or worse, to discredit you behind your back. So stay alert.

ARIES CHEAP SHOTS

- Constantly confronts others
- Sabotages you behind your back
- Sucks up to the VIPs

Learn to Love Them

When an Aries is upset, everyone within earshot will instantly know. A Ram won't fume in silence as Pisces does or withdraw in irritation as Scorpio will. If you work in close proximity, offer empathy. But don't bother bashing his enemy-of-the-moment. An Aries calms down as fast as he flares and can't be bothered with holding a grudge. He's too busy gearing up for the next conquest or confrontation.

With the exception of thoughtful Libra or Cancer, a Ram is first to remember the birthdays, anniversaries, and kids' names of everyone with whom she associates. You'll score points with this colleague if you remember hers with either a card or a small gift.

All in all, getting along with an Aries coworker is uncomplicated. On good days, you'll appreciate her helpfulness and fun-loving exuberance that lightens up the office atmosphere. On bad days, put in your earbuds, turn up the volume on your iPod, and don't make eye contact.

IF YOU ARE AN ARIES

In this world, I call the shots.

MARIAH CAREY (MARCH 27)

You like people, and you take the initiative to introduce yourself at business meetings and after-hours networking mixers. In contrast to any of the Water signs, who usually prefer to sit in the back of the room during meetings and presentations, you like to sit up front and ask lots of questions.

Your self-confidence assures that you'll rarely pass up an opportunity, and you aren't afraid to push yourself outside your comfort zone to get ahead.

So how can you make the 9-to-5 grind work for you?

Stifle the Scandalous Chatter

People gravitate to your friendly, open manner, which makes it easy for you to get them to reveal anything from a personal dilemma to a hot tidbit about the boss. That's why, along with Gemini and Pisces, you are usually first to hear the latest juicy news. What you must learn to resist is indiscriminately blabbing what you know.

A Ram I once knew had a notorious reputation for spreading every rumor as fast as she'd heard it. She was the poster girl for telephone, tele-graph, tell-an-Aries. Once after a semiprivate conversation had turned to more mundane chatter, she literally jumped out of her chair and rushed off to tell her buddies.

Tapping your talent for picking information out of others can be invaluable. If you're trusted not to spread useless grapevine gossip, then you'll be first on the list as a person to confide in when a plum assignment comes up for grabs or a new position is created.

Think Before You Leap into an OTJ Romance

In spite of the sexual harassment laws and company policies designed to prevent love-struck coworkers from hooking up on the job, plenty of people still lock lips before, during, and after working hours. You're one of them.

Flirty, lively, and passionate, you're one of the most romantic signs in the zodiac. You fall fast and hard. Like Gemini, when the fire burns out, you forget just as fast and move on. For that reason it's highly advisable that you avoid thinking of the workplace as your private hunting ground. At the least, you'll ruin your reputation and chances for advancement. At worst, you'll get fired.

If you do tumble into a serious relationship, keep it professional at work. No sly smooches, sexy e-mails, or phone sex on company time, please. And although you're one of the adventurous types, try to resist lunchtime trysts in the supply closet.

Combat Boredom

Your inner kid is quickly bored and always ready to play. You're a fast learner who masters almost anything handed to you in record time. Combine these traits, and you can become an expert with too much time on your hands, which can lead to disaster if you channel your energy into aimless gossip and petty feuds. Because you're good at what you do, you'll expect the boss to protect you and, if necessary, bail you out of trouble. Your bratty behavior might be tolerated longer than most of the other Sun signs, too.

Sooner or later, though, you'll kill your career. First, because you've arrogantly tricked yourself into thinking that you can get away with anything. Second, because it will become less painful for the boss to replace you than to keep covering your butt.

If you regularly have time on your hands, ask your boss for more responsibility. Attend in-house education forums. They're free, and you'll be perceived as interested in your company while furthering your future as well. Plus, don't forget your coworkers. Offering to help out an overworked colleague will instantly add positive bonus points to your reputation.

FROM FED UP TO FIRED UP

If I set my mind to something, I do it.

VICTORIA BECKHAM (APRIL 17)

You're the zodiac's rule breaker; the word *can't* doesn't exist in your vocabulary; and, like Gemini, Sagittarius, and Leo, you'll try anything once. Your philosophy is to do something, even if it's wrong, rather than stand on the sidelines. Your personal challenge lies in knowing how to control and focus your forceful nature to ensure that you come out on top without earning a bad reputation along the way.

Pick Your Battles

This is crucial, Aries, if you plan to become anything more than just another working slob. Your first instinct is to argue over the slightest issue that you deem unfair or unworkable. If you assail everyone you meet over every triviality, you'll slide down the list of up-and-comers faster than a nit-picking Virgo can gripe her way into the unemployment line. No matter how justified you may feel, arbitrary power struggles will make you look overbearing and mean-spirited.

Stop and think before you flare because you didn't get consulted over the office color scheme or argue with your boss over every assignment. Count to ten. Assess the situation. Ask yourself is this a career-threatening issue or just an annoyance.

Anger breeds anger. If you're continually pissed off, you can't possibly be effective in your work or feel good about your job. Control your temper, unleashing it in a professional manner (no shouting or pencil cup tossing) and as rarely as possible, and you'll become a formidable force instead of just another office hothead.

Know When to Quit

Unlike some signs, your problem isn't hanging onto a mundane job long past its pull date. Your hindrance to getting ahead is the opposite: You can be too willing to job jump without a plan.

A former Aries coworker of mine has gone through countless career changes but has yet, at well past forty, to stay committed to a job longer than a few years. At the company where we worked, in less than three years she had transferred to three different departments and applied for yet another internal move, which she was refused. Her downfall, as is the downfall of many Rams, is a restless nature, plus a penchant for repeatedly jumping first and discovering, too late, that she'd only substituted one unsatisfactory situation for another.

TIPS FOR SUCCESS

- Write down what you want
- Create an action plan
- Take your time scouting out your options

Instead of making a lateral move either to another department or a different company, take time to look for a position that offers more money, better benefits, or a greater opportunity. Anything less, and you're committing self-sabotage by giving in to your impulsive nature. Save yourself a headache and stick with the job you have until you find one that truly meets your needs and desires. While you're searching for a better job, milk the one you have for all it's worth. Grab every chance to learn new skills, cross train in other areas, and sign up for any freebie educational benefits offered.

Ace an Interview

Your natural exuberance and disarming smile instantly put you among the top candidates. You are renowned for convincing anyone that you're the right person for the job, which can give you an edge. However, you can just as easily oversell and talk yourself into and out of a job offer before the interview gets started.

Some Aries raise their voices when they are excited. If you're one of them, consciously practice speaking in a quiet tone. Stand in front of a mirror or enlist the help of a friend, partner, or your spouse.

As does Gemini, you're inclined to skip digging for details in favor of skimming the facts. But when going after your dream job, you'll make a better impression if you've thoroughly studied the company and mention what appealed to you about working there in the interview.

Restraint is your key to making a good impression. Although you like to take charge, let the interviewer set the pace, or you'll seem pushy. And stifle any urges to show up the interviewer by trying to prove that you're smarter than him or her. Maybe you are, but since that person is in control, insulting his or her intelligence isn't the smartest thing to do.

Aries-Friendly Careers

You need a job that doesn't tie you down, either physically (to a desk doing the same routine tasks) or creatively (where you don't get the opportunity to unlock your imagination).

Astrology tells us that, because you are ruled by fiery Mars, you're well suited for dangerous careers such as firefighter, soldier, or metallurgist. While this might be true for some Aries, it's also silly to think that every Ram wants to put him- or herself in harm's way any more than any other Sun sign would.

What your fiery nature demands is independent action. Whether you have a desk job that requires you to travel or you telecommute from home, the best careers for you are ones that give you lots of independence, let you use your talent for innovation, and take risks.

The following are a few possibilities.

Entrepreneur

Whether it's the neighborhood hair salon, car repair shop, or a chain of clothing stores, owning your own business appeals to your need for independence, as well as your inner risk taker.

Futurist

Combining your ability to play a hunch with your innovative imagination could keep you interested as you predict what the public will need and want in the future as a big-business consultant.

Executive Assistant

Working independently, making decisions in the boss's absence, and/or supervising other clerical staff keeps you on your toes.

Public Relations Agent

Extolling your clients' virtues and protecting them against negative publicity should appeal to your natural talent for exaggeration. Bonus: You get to talk a lot.

Skip Tracer / Bounty Hunter

Whether you work from home on your computer or travel across the country hot on a bail jumper's trail, tracking down deadbeats and bad guys appeals to your inner hero.

CHAPTER THREE

Taurus
April 20–May 20

Element:	Earth
Quality:	Fixed
Symbol:	The Bull
Ruler:	Venus
Key word:	Conscientious
Work-a-tude:	What's the bottom line?

INSTANT INSIGHTS

I don't want to be alone; I want to be left alone.

AUDREY HEPBURN (MAY 4)

Taurus is Feminine Fixed Earth, the sign of patience, stability, and steady progress. Dedicated to family, friends, and their employers, Bulls are trustworthy, dependable, and practical.

Taurus is like the house of bricks in the children's fairytale *The Three Little Pigs*. Huff and puff all you want; nothing will move a Bull but the Bull himself. This sign is the least likely to throw caution to the wind in any aspect of life.

Mutable Earth Virgo negotiates and Cardinal Earth Capricorn will take a calculated risk, but Fixed Earth Taurus natives like a sure thing. These diligent people are creatures of habit who thrive on structure and schedules. Bulls hate change. Never forget this important fact, because this single trait is both this sign's key to success and its Achilles' heel.

That's why she can get stuck in a career that's far beneath her abilities and talents. She reaches a comfort zone that isn't exactly a dream life or job, but it offers the security that every Taurus craves.

Ruled by luxury-loving Venus and anchored in the money and values Second House, the Bull is more than capable of getting everything she wants in life. Venus also rules Libra. Libra inherited Venus's desire to be the most popular kid on the block, while Taurus inherited her love of creature comforts. Money is only a means to an end for a Taurus, however. The possessions it buys are the fabric that weaves this sign's personal safety net.

The Bull's Feminine nature bestows a certain gentle manner to even the burliest guy, and astrology paints the Taurus native as serene and peace loving. This makes the Bull a pushover, right? Wrong! Push a real bull, and he'll charge. Push a human version, and you're likely to end up the target of a bellowing verbal onslaught. Don't confuse this with a hotheaded Ram's penchant for routinely flying off the handle. Luckily, a Bull rarely charges without provocation. When he does, you'll think you're in a ten-scale earthquake.

Fixed Air Aquarians focus on abstract ideas. They will talk your ears off to convince you they are right. Fixed Water Scorpios crave emotional security and have an assortment of tests to subject you to before you win their trust. Fixed Fire Leos need to be the center of a world where everyone else relies on them. But Fixed Earth Bulls want to see solid results of their efforts—the balanced budget, the well-built home, the safe landing.

TAURUS ON THE JOB

You don't want to push the person doing the work because you will affect the quality.

CHRIS BROWN (MAY 5)

Ever seen a real bull being led by its nose ring? Sometimes it follows along, docile as can be. Other times it plants its hooves, and the person leading has no choice but to stop until the bull decides to move again. The human version is eerily similar.

There's no doubt that Taurus is one of the hardest workers in the zodiac. The catch is that, along with Scorpio and Virgo, urging a Taurus to speed up practically guarantees a slowdown. Jack Nicholson has been quoted as saying, "Every director implored me, 'Jack, can't you talk a little bit faster?' It was like a hot button for me, and I would become hateful." You can bet that the *harder, faster, beat-the-clock* approach that whips other signs into shape won't work on a Bull.

While money motivates a Taurus because it equals security, the key to winning one's loyalty is to show that you value him on a personal as well as a professional basis.

Managing a Bull
Be Consistent

Reliable, practical Bulls need a stable work routine. That includes regular reviews, raises, and vacations. Aries may love the excitement of chasing a big deal, but Taurus loves closing it and depositing the check. Expect your Taurus assistant to constantly put up with an irregular schedule, irrational coworkers, or irritating customers, and she'll turn into a sullen grouch who can't get her work done on time. Put her in a quiet spot, stick a green plant on her desk, and give her a set routine, and she'll morph into an efficient whiz who can outwork anyone else in the office. Including a pile-it-on Sagittarius.

The Bull is one of the best people to have around in a crisis. He'll keep his head while everyone else runs in circles. What this sign won't put up with is a chronically hectic environment. He hates commotion. Never blindside your Bull salesman by sending him out unprepared. Cold calling on potential clients might be bold Leo's cup of tea, but the Bull isn't a natural schmoozer. His sales philosophy is usually, "Here's the product. Buy it, or don't."

FAMOUS TAURUS MONEY MAKERS

- James Dyson, creator of the high-tech Dyson vacuums (May 2)
- George Lucas, producer/director (May 14)
- Dietrich Mateschitz, cofounder of Red Bull energy drink (May 20)

Keep Them Enthused

If you want a job done well, give it to a Taurus. Bulls have the ability to focus with a single-mindedness that rivals a Capricorn on the hunt for a corner office, and they don't need hand-holding as a Cancer might. You can rely on them in a pinch and be comfortable leaving one in charge when you're away on a business trip.

That's because a Taurus doesn't work for you. He works for himself. He doesn't need an office mom or view his workplace as a dating pool. What he wants is respect, praise, a few perks to make him feel appreciated—and to keep steadily moving up the company ladder.

Be as liberal as you can with bonuses, stock options, and raises. Keep her motivated with a plan for advancement, and be honest. There's no faster way to lose this employee than to try to string her along with empty promises.

Everyone loves a perk, but thoughtful personal gestures make a huge impact on a Venus-ruled Taurus. Have two tickets to the theater you can't use? Offer them to her, or let her leave early to beat the traffic (with pay, of course) if she's going out of town for the weekend.

As a rule, Bulls desire long-term stability. With straightforward guidance, a plan to help them grow, and sincere encouragement, they'll stick with you through thick and thin and do a near-perfect job along the way.

Read the Warning Signs

Conscientious Taurus wants to do the best job possible. Any hint that you think she's not capable feeds her near-morbid fear of being thought stupid.

Further, an exaggerated sense of pride that's fueled by an inner insecurity can prevent her from asking for assistance.

Whether a craftsperson or the CEO of a Fortune 500 corporation, her approach to work is precise and habitual. When change happens, give her as much lead time as possible. Provide clear guidelines, plenty of access to you, and a fixed schedule to keep a Bull contented and productive.

When a Taurus is frustrated, she mumbles one-word answers. If she's overwhelmed, she might avoid you while she tries to figure out how to handle the load. You have to step in. It could take some probing, but if you approach her in a nonthreatening way, she'll usually open up. Never act superior. A Bull doesn't shrug off other people's condescending attitudes like a Pisces would. If she thinks that you are putting her down, she'll never trust you again.

As for that famous temper, Taurus doesn't whine over every little slight like a Libra might or spew a laundry-list of grievances as Virgo can. Bulls hold their anger in until they snap. Stave off a flare-up by checking in with this employee through regular meetings and friendly drop-ins, especially during times of change.

Surviving Boss Bull
Know What You're Dealing With

A Libra boss will appreciate your input. A Sagittarius boss will chat with you over coffee. A Taurus boss, however, wants things done his way. Period.

Nagging to get your idea on the table might wear down a Pisces boss, but asking once is enough for a Bull. Even if he likes your proposal, he'll take twice as long as most other bosses to decide whether or not to give his approval.

A by-the-book Bull takes a dim view of blind leaps into new ventures. Like Cancer, she believes in well-thought-out plans and carefully considered options. Unlike Fixed Fire Leo, the Bull isn't after a fast buck. If you have a knack for sniffing out hot opportunities at bargain prices or can find a way to shave 15 percent off the office supply budget, you'll earn her admiration.

Keep your desk clean and dress appropriately for your job. He's ruled by Venus, and appearances are important. You don't have to max out your credit card, but, whether you're a mechanic or a junior executive, being neat and well groomed earns bonus points with this boss.

Boss Bull isn't a back-slapping wheeler-dealer or prone to taking risks trying to double his money. He believes in safeguarding the company and loves watching the sales and profit climb at a constant pace.

Be Reliable

Nothing impresses a Taurus more than showing her that you are stable, honest, and dependable, unless you add a talent for making money. Having all four of those virtues could earn you a partnership in record time.

Remember, Boss Bull hates change. Bull Bill Hewlett, cofounder of Hewlett-Packard, said that he wanted "a company built on a loyal and dedicated staff." So does your Taurus boss. It takes too much effort to continually hire and train new people. And too much money.

Boss Bull lives by the old saying, *"An honest day's work for an honest day's pay."* While he won't blatantly stand over your shoulder as a Capricorn boss would, don't think he won't notice if you take too many long lunches or slide into your desk ten minutes late most days. Boss Bull has an internal calculator that clicks each time you slack off. Each click means that you've taken money (his money) that you haven't earned.

Once the total gets too high, he'll call you on your bad behavior. If you're lucky and he values your work, you'll get off with a warning. One is all you'll get.

TAURUS WORDS TO LIVE BY

"I still look at myself and want to improve."
—David Beckham (May 2)

"If you don't ask, you don't get."
—Stevie Wonder (May 13)

Expect to Work Your Butt Off

Work is your key word. I had a Taurus boss who never raised his voice. He was kind, soft-spoken, and paid his employees well. However, his idea of a perfect day at the office was that no one went home until the job was done. Yours might not be this demanding, but every Boss Bull will expect you to earn your salary.

Don't try to wow him by turning in six less-than-perfect projects that you rushed through at the last minute. He's much more impressed by a consistent flow of professional-quality work. Plus, it irritates him to have to correct your typos.

Taurus respects responsibility, tradition, and loyalty. Show an interest in the company, read the year-end reports, and be frugal in your use of everything from sick time to paper clips. Helping your Taurus boss keep an eye on the bottom line wins her respect.

Think of it like this: There are no guarantees in business, but when the economy gets tough, this tough boss is likely to have the cash reserves and cautious investments to see you and the company through the crisis.

Coping with a Taurus Coworker

Your Taurus colleague's Fixed nature makes this native feel as if he or she should be able to handle anything alone. That's why a Bull will rarely ask for help. *Be tough. Be strong. Don't let them see you sweat.* This is the Taurus approach to both work and life. But beneath the persevering face they show to the world, Bulls can be as sensitive as a Water sign.

Be Friendly

Despite a reputation for being dogged, stubborn, and opinionated, a Bull is also shy. The best way to break the ice with a new Taurus colleague is to make her feel welcome by introducing her to your coworkers and giving her a tour her through the office. If you don't take the initiative, she might never meet anyone. Unlike an Air sign that quickly makes friends, the Bull needs time to get to know you. If you're the newbie in the group, ask her for a few pointers. She'll think you're smart for knowing that she has the answers. And she does.

While no one is resistant to a juicy piece of gossip, Taurus usually isn't interested unless it's either aimed at her or is insider news that she can use to further her career. Ask about her family or hobby and share your own stories. She'll warm up a lot faster. You won't regret taking the time to make this coworker an ally. Once a Taurus decides that she likes you, she'll always stand up for you and watch your back.

Keep Your Guard Up

Real bulls are territorial. So are human ones. If your Taurus coworker thinks that you're trying to muscle in on a project or have your eye on her cozy, corner desk, she'll instantly go into protective mode. This can include anything from politely distancing herself from your attempts to chat to refusing to work with you in any way whatsoever.

A Bull who's after your job has the endurance of a cat after a mouse. She'll wait and watch before making a move. She'll try to sabotage you by slacking off so that you bear the brunt of a project or purposely "forgetting" to include important facts. Then, when you're fumbling around, she'll step in with the crucial information to make herself look good in front of the boss.

She's also the champion grudge holder in the zodiac. Even a Scorpio can't stand up to a Taurus who feels that she's been betrayed. Taurus can spend years trying to make you look bad every chance she gets. Fortunately, it takes a lot to push the average Bull to this extreme.

Show her you're as tough as she is by speaking up when she tries to dominate the meeting or conversation. Use e-mail to ask for her input on joint tasks, keep confidential information locked up, and always watch your back.

TAURUS CHEAP SHOTS

- Uses intimidation to win
- Holds a grudge
- Withholds critical information

Learn to Love Them

Bulls are some of the easiest people to get along with in the workforce. They're usually team players and are too busy building their careers to get caught up in ordinary office politics.

Respect his space. Just as at home, Taurus on the job "owns" his desk, his pencil cup, and his sticky notes. Virgos can get obsessive about where everything goes—inbox to the right, phone to the left. A Bull considers anything that's in his cubicle or office his personal property. So don't borrow anything without asking.

Most Bulls aren't too chatty, but they all love food. Inviting your coworker to lunch is a good way to engage her in a friendly conversation. Offering to help when you see that she's overloaded is another. She won't forget the gesture.

Most Bulls have an earthy sense of humor that pops up unexpectedly, and like Capricorn, they get gloomy on a regular basis. You can turn this sign into a pal by laughing at his jokes when he's feeling lively and keeping chocolate in your desk to toss at him when he's down.

IF YOU ARE A TAURUS

My theory is that, if you look confident, you can pull anything off—even if you have no clue what you're doing.

JESSICA ALBA (APRIL 28)

You are self-reliant and fearless. You're naturally suspicious of glad-handing types who make big promises. Instead of blindly jumping into a situation as a Fire sign would, you prefer to take the wait-and-see approach. Metaphorically speaking, you can take a lump-of-coal project and turn it into a diamond-producing success. This is because you don't lose patience as a Gemini would or get bogged down in the details as a Virgo can.

You can be counted on in a pinch and will work as long and hard as it takes to get the job done.

So how can you make your career go from so-so to sensational?

Learn to Kick Your Own Ass

You have talent, drive, and ambition. However, because you're a Fixed sign, your first reaction is to stay put. Plus, your bullish penchant for immediately sinking into a worst-case scenario kills your enthusiasm. You'll use any excuse from not wanting to uproot the family to the bird-in-the-hand philosophy to avoid taking a risk. You get rut-bound because as long as you get an annual raise and a few perks, you fool yourself into thinking that's enough. Sooner or later, though, you'll get a case of the chronic complaints. Nothing's right. You'll bitch and whine because you know you've settled for less than you can achieve.

The late comedian George Carlin, a Taurus, said, "Think off-center." Make this your mantra. Once you learn that everything isn't black or white, you'll find that you have all kinds of options. Set small goals that force you to move outside your comfort zone. Network with people who can help your career or find a mentor.

If you want to grow, you eventually have to take the leap. Everything's a risk, and, yes, you might fail. But you can always find another routine job. If you don't try, you'll never get anywhere.

Issue a Storm Warning

A Sagittarius temper is like a blast of dynamite—sudden, loud, and over in an instant. An upset Capricorn grumbles and bitches. You let annoyance build slowly but steadily until you erupt like Mount St. Helens. The initial blast shocks everyone around you into silence. Then you belch out a lava flow of everything that's bothered you since the day you were hired. By the time an explosion happens, it's usually too late. You'll either toss your keys on the boss's desk and walk out, or you'll get escorted to your car by security.

This natural reluctance to deal with issues as they arise can kill your career. Handle them when they happen. Addressing problems as they crop up is smart. In the long run it saves everyone trouble. Especially you.

That goes for talking to the boss, too. If you think you deserve more money at review time, go prepared with a list of your accomplishments. You'll be armed with something other than your Taurus righteous indignation, which won't buy you a burger. When you lose your cool, you're the only one who really loses.

Take off Your Blinders

Sure, you crank out the work. But turning yourself into a cubicle robot won't get you anywhere. You can be so focused on day-to-day tasks that you miss opportunities to learn new things—or get blindsided by a rival who's after your job.

Make time to keep up with changes. Read the company newsletter. Have brief weekly meetings with your supervisor, and volunteer to sit on a committee or join a team that's working on a new project.

You don't have to spread gossip to make the grapevine work for you. Listening to the news can keep you in touch with what's going on in the company. Make friends with colleagues in other departments. This network can help you be the first to know when a plum assignment or promotion is coming up.

Expanding your world at work will help you to avoid a backstabber, earn a rep as a go-getter, and give you a boost up the corporate ladder.

TIPS FOR SUCCESS

- Set achievable goals outside your comfort zone
- Research your options
- Act instead of react

FROM FED UP TO FIRED UP

I'm always interested in people who depart from what is expected of them and go into new territory.

CATE BLANCHETT (MAY 14)

You're one of the most powerful signs in the zodiac. Creative and smart, your natural willpower can help you achieve anything you desire. When you're on a mission, nothing can stop you.

Being both a Feminine (receptive) sign and ruled by Venus makes you sensitive to the moods and emotions swirling around you—especially negative ones. As if you don't have enough rolling around in your own head, when you listen to the office whiners bitch about how bad things are, you can fall into a funk. Your challenge is to ignore the pessimism and focus your energy in a positive way.

Cut through the Crap

One of the worst ways to sabotage your own career is your willingness to buy into every scary scenario that spews out of the rumor mill. Instead of digging for the facts, you can assume the worst and retreat behind your desk. Keeping your head down in tough times is one thing. Allowing yourself to be ruled by worry can be paralyzing.

The quickest way to cut through the B.S. is to ask questions. Follow up on persistent rumors with your boss. Confront the office gossip and ask her where she got her facts. Most of the time these steps will be enough to pop your doom-and-gloom balloon.

Know When to Quit

There's an old saying, "When you snooze, you lose."

When worried about your job, your first instinct is to retreat instead of charge. I've known Bulls who would rather take a demotion than quit because of anxiety over making a change. Hanging on until you're the last employee out the door might seem safe, but sit in a stale job too long, and you will lose the competitive edge that you need to stay ahead of the game.

Along with Pisces and Virgo, fear disguised as procrastination is one of your biggest obstacles to getting ahead. If you're not moving up and you can't make yourself move out, sooner or later you'll be tossed out. Settling for less than you can achieve sends a signal to the boss that you might not be the asset she thought you were.

One way to combat your concerns is to be prepared. Keep your résumé updated. Read the classifieds and visit the Web sites of companies that seem like a good match. Once you see that you have options, you'll start to relax, feel more secure, and be able to move forward.

Ace an Interview

Your friendly demeanor, firm handshake, and professional appearance make a great first impression. You know that you're well qualified and able to handle any job, and you need to get those facts imprinted on an interviewer's mind.

One way you earn negative points is by making the person you're talking with pull every word out of you. Unlike a glib Gemini dropping names or a nervous Pisces reliving his life story, when you're under pressure you can clam up tighter than a Cancer in a snit. To help yourself relax, approach the process as you would a friendly conversation.

Be prepared with two or three queries about the job you're applying for, such as the responsibilities of the position and the organizational structure. Arm yourself with a few facts about the company and discuss them. Companies like candidates who are interested in more than just a paycheck.

Speaking of paychecks, although pay scales and benefits are two of your prime motivators, this stuff isn't usually discussed in a first interview unless you're applying to be a Wal-Mart greeter. Negotiating those areas comes *after* you've been offered the job.

Smile. Some Bulls stiffen and look stern when they're stressed. If you're one of them, remember tension is contagious. You don't want to make the interviewer so uncomfortable that he crosses you off the list before you get started.

Combat the jitters with the old standby, deep breathing exercises, before you arrive or while you wait. And think positive thoughts, Bully. You can ace anything once you decide you can.

Taurus-Friendly Careers

Astrology teaches us that with Venus as your ruling planet, you're one of the creative signs. This doesn't mean that every Taurus will end up in the arts, but you will add an inspired touch to any career you choose. You're great at working either independently or as part of a team, which puts you ahead of most people from the start. Above all, you need a job that acts as an anchor from which you can expand your talent.

The following are several possibilities.

Fund-Raiser

You can smell money a mile away and have a natural talent for instilling guilt into rich patrons to extract the max from them for a good cause.

Foodie

Whether you're a food critic telling people what to eat, a chef in your own restaurant preparing hearty meals with ingredients fresh from your garden, or a bakery owner inventing decadent desserts, food is a natural win-win business for you. Bonus: You get to eat the leftovers.

Landscape Designer

Your artistic flair allows you to create lush lawns and gardens that add value as well as beauty to a home or business. This job appeals to your love for both nature and a good investment.

Animal Cop

Fighting for those who can't fight for themselves makes you a perfect candidate to save helpless animals from abuse.

Lawyer

Your demand for justice is soul deep. Whether you're prosecuting, defending, or getting the best divorce deal for a client, you love to argue an opponent into the ground.

CHAPTER FOUR

Gemini
May 21–June 20

Element:	Air
Quality:	Mutable
Symbol:	The Twins
Ruler:	Mercury
Key word:	Flexible
Work-a-tude:	Keep me busy.

INSTANT INSIGHTS

The world belongs to the energetic.

RALPH WALDO EMERSON (MAY 25)

Masculine Mutable Air Gemini is inquisitive, clever, and tolerant.
They make friends everywhere they go and can motivate others with their contagious enthusiasm. Twins are team players who crave variety and need constant challenges to keep them committed.

Ruled by Mercury, the Olympic champ of networking, and located within the Third House of communication, the Twin is a people person and usually a great conversationalist. Don't confuse this with Libra's talent for mindless small talk. Gemini is like an information sieve, always gathering, processing, and spitting out ideas.

A Twin is like the classic cartoon character, Road Runner, always outsmarting the coyote and too fast to catch. This talent is also Gemini's downfall. When blended with the tendency to scatter his ambitions, sometimes the only person he outsmarts is himself.

FAMOUS VERSATILE GEMINI

- Steffi Graf, dubbed the best woman tennis player of all time because of her ability to play equally well on any surface (June 14)
- Sir Paul McCartney, former Beatle and musical legend (June 18)
- Angelina Jolie, movie star, philanthropist, and humanitarian (June 4)

Fortunately, whether it's cleaning house or brainstorming a marketing plan in a bleak economy, the majority of your Gemini coworkers are fun to be around. They can turn a boring or daunting task into a successful mission accomplished through their optimism and resourcefulness.

Gemini tempers are short-lived but caustic. Second only to a really pissed Scorpio, they can verbally cut you to shreds. Because of a blind-to-their-own-faults talent for rationalization, some Twins seldom apologize in words. If they feel bad about their outburst, you can expect a small gift or extra compliments and attention the next time they see you.

Astrology teaches us that Gemini natives are born with a high degree of intelligence. However, it's not the deep intellect of Aquarius or the philosophical leaning of Sagittarius. Twins are speedy learners who pick up the nuts and bolts of the task or project without trying to master it, as would a more thorough Virgo. The Twin can't be bothered. There's too much to learn and too little time.

Twins have a never-ending curiosity to push the envelope. This doesn't mean they can't focus on a long-term goal or study profound subjects. But you can bet that while other medical students are sleeping on their weekends off, the Gemini doctor-to-be is learning how to sky dive or getting a minor in creative writing.

Mutable Fire Sagittarius often rambles about everyday minutia. Mutable Earth Virgo has a nervous energy that turns into critical observations. Mutable Water Pisces conversations can focus on emotional turmoil. Gemini, however, is like a breath of fresh air. She can replace stale views with original ideas and liven up a dull lunch meeting with an inexhaustible supply of entertaining anecdotes. A Twin takes people at face value, has a child's sense of trust, and has a gift for talking anyone, including herself, into just about anything.

GEMINI ON THE JOB

If you want a guarantee, buy a toaster.
CLINT EASTWOOD (MAY 31)

To say that a Gemini is easily bored is like saying a Libra can take a while to make up her mind. Lively Gemini needs plenty of people contact and mental challenges to stay enthused about anything, including work.

This colleague is competent and, usually, one step ahead of everyone else. The multitasking abilities that astrology assigns a Twin are genuine. The downside is that this original jack-of-all-trades is also notorious for a lack of follow-through. Other signs will research the details, but a Twin only wants to wrap up the project, the sale, or the meeting as quickly as possible and move on to the next task.

Every Gemini wants to help, even if it's thinking up a better way to sort the company mail. Earn his loyalty by welcoming his ideas. Sometimes he'll bombard you with his views, and his suggestions won't always work. But look at it this way—at least you have an employee or colleague who is interested in making his, and your, workplace run smoother.

Managing a Twin
Be Flexible
Sticking a Gemini in a corner with routine tasks is as big a disaster as relegating an Aries to the back office—with one huge difference. Where the

Ram will become a bored goof-off, an enterprising Twin will get her work done and have time left to research, start, and run a private side business on your time and money. She figures that if you aren't smart enough to make the most of her talents, that's your loss.

A Twin needs room to breathe in life and in her job. You can help by giving her some leeway. If possible, let her vary the time she goes to lunch or on break. If you can't have a true open-door policy, the next best thing is to have several brief and informal chats a week. Warning: Set a time limit. As with Virgo and Sagittarius, Gemini is famous for monopolizing the conversation. Let her experiment with different ways to do her job, offer a variety of tasks, and keep the communication flowing. You'll end up with a smart, charming pro who will excel in a diverse range of duties.

Keep Them Enthused

The Twins of Gemini are more than just an astrological symbol. A properly motivated Twin is a brainstorming whiz who can work circles around any two other employees.

Airy Gemini needs constant stimulation. If you want to keep her around long enough to earn her first two-week vacation, you must keep her interested. Don't panic. This isn't as difficult as you might have heard. Yes, a Twin loves change. The secret is that it's change within structure. Even with a reputation for being fickle, this native is not a true job hopper. She prefers to hop around a familiar environment. She'll thrive in a fast-paced spot where she can figure out a way to save a presentation, appease a client, or track down a lost shipment. Or, put her in charge of testing new procedures and processes.

She can handle the phone, fax, computer, and greet clients all at the same time—if she feels like it. Don't confuse this with a Cancer's varying moods. A Twin has a changeable nature. Something that appeals today is history tomorrow. She might love showing newbies the ropes one week and think it's not worth her time the next because another project's caught her attention.

Gemini is the human version of a breezy day. He was made to circulate ideas. Put your Gemini in a think tank where his try-anything attitude often inspires surprisingly simple solutions to complex issues. Let him move within the company or work in a central area dispensing information, and you'll get a walking information source that can fill in anywhere.

Beware the Double Speak

Lying comes as naturally to a Gemini as flirting. You've heard of the proverbial salesman who could sell refrigerators at the Arctic Circle? A Twin can do that, plus sell igloos in Louisiana.

Although it can be designed to discredit a rival, most Twins use this gift to buy time. First, to convince you that he can handle a job, no matter what his qualifications. Second, for when he needs to cover his butt. When on a roll, this sign can be as convincing as a Washington lobbyist pushing pork.

Unfortunately, even if you've known a Twin for years, you can't always spot when one is bending the truth. That's why it's crucial to hold her accountable. Instead of accepting a verbal update, ask for progress reports.

A Twin usually appreciates firm but fair guidance. It helps him learn better time management skills. Sometimes, you'll lose one who's unwilling to cooperate. A quiet Gemini is getting ready to bolt. The communication stops. He withdraws to his office and ignores you and everyone else. If he's been an asset, offer as much as you can to get him to stay. Chances are he doesn't want to leave in the first place, and if you can compromise, you'll both win.

Surviving Boss Twin

Know What You're Dealing With

A Virgo boss demands attention to detail. The Aquarius boss expects you to keep up on the newest trends. A Gemini boss, however, operates in hot-off-the-press mode, and so should you.

Routine makes her nervous, and if things get too comfy, she's perfectly capable of turning the office upside down in order to create her version of excitement.

True to his Twin nature, this boss can be charming one day, then snappy the next. The good news is that his irritability won't last long. He's neither as moody as Cancer nor as grumpy as Capricorn. However, when he's on a tirade, his caustic tongue can sting. Fortunately, most of his barbs won't be aimed at you. Keep it that way by keeping your head down when he has an outburst.

Twins admire innovativeness and intelligence. Read the trade journals for your industry and discuss relevant issues with her. Don't be afraid to make far-out suggestions, as this boss likes to consider all the possibilities. Keep her calendar updated and give her fifteen-, ten-, and five-minute warnings before a client appears.

This boss believes in *"Nothing ventured, nothing gained"* and thrives on creating changes that keep her department or company on the cutting edge.

Be Fast on Your Feet

To impress a Gemini boss, you have to be quick on the uptake and able to switch gears in a heartbeat. She might ask you drop what you're doing to set up a luncheon for fifty of her closest business associates by day after tomorrow.

The quickest way to win his approval is to be the resource person for this resourceful boss. Keep your PDA crammed with contact information for people whom you can call in any situation. He'll skim the trade magazines. You read them. Clip interesting articles or be able to find the information online.

GEMINI WORDS TO LIVE BY

"Conformity is the jailer of freedom."
—John F. Kennedy (May 29)

"I think the thing to do is enjoy the ride while you're on it."
—Johnny Depp (June 9)

She'll encourage you to attend business luncheons and after-hours networking events, as long as you keep bringing back insider tips or the latest news about cutting-edge technologies. A Gemini believes in education, and if you're pursuing a degree, Boss Twin will often agree to be flexible with your work schedule.

You might have to take extra vitamins to keep up with this human whirlwind, but the free education you get from just being around a Gemini boss is well worth the trouble.

Expect Contradictions

If you want logic, work for an Aquarius. Your Gemini boss will act like the company efficiency expert one day and won't know whether you're working or surfing the Net the next. He'll ditch a brainstorm you've been jamming on for a week and won't care how many steps the project took or how much it disrupts the office.

Unlike a Capricorn, who checks her facts and then outlines an action plan, Boss Gemini has flashes of insight and thinks in sound bytes. Her desk will be papered with yellow sticky notes covered with cryptic scribbles. She's great at delegating, so you get the busywork. In the meantime, she's spotted another idea buried under a stack of papers and immediately forgets the first idea—the one you're slaving over. The weird thing is that the office manages to keep running efficiently most of the time.

Working for a Gemini is frustrating, because you never quite know what to expect when you get to work. It's also exhilarating, because you're practically guaranteed that you'll never be bored.

Coping with a Gemini Coworker

A vivacious Gemini livens up any office. This friendly, helpful colleague will introduce you to everyone and is happy to show you around the office. If a Gemini likes you, it takes about sixty seconds for her to become your new BFF. Don't count on a lifetime relationship, however; once you know the ropes, she'll be off to help the next new hire get acquainted.

Assume Nothing

Pinning down a Gemini is like trying to trap the wind in a bucket. She processes information by zeroing in on what she wants to hear, then mixes it up with what would be her perfect scenario and spits out a Gemini-truth. "The boss said I was perfect for the supervisor position." What the boss *might* have said was, "Post this supervisor job requisition on the bulletin board. If you're interested in applying, the instructions are on the reverse."

To be fair, she convinces herself that's what the boss said, or at least meant, because she assumes that she can read between the lines. Reading between her lines isn't so simple. Pointed questions don't always work. She knows what you want, but by the time the words spill out, it will be an abbreviated version or, worse, a one-word answer that only leads you to having to ask yet another question. As much as a Twin can talk, true communication can be like trying to pry a secret out of a Scorpio. So always dig for the facts yourself.

Keep Your Guard Up

Anything you say can and will be used against you. Keep this in mind anytime you feel the need to confide in, or gossip with, a Gemini. Don't confuse this with a gossipy Ram who wants to be the first to tell a juicy story.

A ruthless Twin deliberately plays both sides of the fence. She'll gossip to you about a colleague, then gossip *about* you to someone else. She can twist an innocent remark out of context or use a remark you made against you.

This Twin operates on rumor and innuendo, dropping hints that he has important information. Or he'll bombard you with questions designed to make you feel unsure of yourself. It's wise to listen more than you talk and limit your side of the conversation to mundane subjects. If you have a run-in with a double-dealing Twin, let him know that you know he's the culprit. He'll lie through his teeth to deny it, but that's okay. You've made your point that you're no pushover.

GEMINI CHEAP SHOTS

- Lies
- Plays both sides against each other
- Bombards you with questions designed to make you unsure of yourself

Learn to Love Them

Who wouldn't like a Gemini? One of the natural flirts of the zodiac, even a Twin on the verge of retirement can charm a smile out of the surliest Capricorn or steal the spotlight from a Leo holding court.

A Twin is a people person. She gets restless no matter what she's doing, so invite her to go shopping at lunch. She'll appreciate getting out of the office. You'll have to keep track of the time, though, as most Gemini aren't clock watchers.

Unlike a possessive Taurus or suspicious Cancer, your Gemini office mate has a "*what's mine is yours*" attitude. She freely shares her supplies, time, and knowledge. Make her a close work pal and a great source of information by sharing yours, too.

IF YOU ARE A GEMINI

Chaos is a friend of mine.

BOB DYLAN (MAY 24)

There isn't a boss you can't charm or a colleague you can't win over. You rarely lose an argument, and you're willing to work as long as it takes to get a job done.

You're terrific at spitting out ideas and thinking up ingenious solutions to problems or quick fixes for a last-minute crisis. Time means nothing to you when you're engrossed in one of your pet projects, and you're not afraid to speak up for yourself, or to speak out if you think that something's unfair.

So how can you thrive, not just survive, in the workplace?

Govern Your Tabloid Tongue

While you can be a walking encyclopedia of information, the downside is that you can also come across as an easily distracted motor-mouth. You can drop as many names as a Capricorn trying to impress, or turn into a nonstop torrent of information like an Aquarius on a rant. But instead of amazing anyone with your knowledge, you come across as a clueless airhead.

Like Aries and Libra, you love the office grapevine. While most of you Twins are neither as blatant as a Ram rushing to be the first to spread a juicy story nor as critical as a Libra putting down a rival, you definitely have a hard time keeping a secret. You also jump to conclusions, which causes you to embellish facts, making what you pass along much worse than what you heard. If you want to seriously succeed, you must learn to zip your lips.

TIPS FOR SUCCESS

- Manage your time
- Finish one project before moving to the next
- Control the gossip

Learn to Say No

Biting off more than you can chew is a soul trait of every Gemini on the planet.

It's true that you can usually do twice the work in half the time of most people. However, when you simultaneously tell the boss that the project you've barely started is almost finished and assure your coworker that you'll wrap up her assignment so she can leave early, you get in trouble. Why? Because that talent you have for stretching the truth gets turned inward. You lie to yourself, and you believe the lie.

Part of the reason you continue to pack your plate with too much work is that you think someone might get the upper hand should you turn down a task. Part is fear that your boss or colleague might think you're not pulling your weight. However, turning down a project or asking for more time to finish a task isn't half as bad as being so overloaded that nothing gets accomplished.

Time management skills are key to keeping your head above water. Take a workshop, or sign up for an online time-tracking service. Once you learn the difference between real time and Gemini time, you'll begin to rescue yourself from overtime.

Control Your Crush Rush

The fastest way to be taken off the up-and-comer list is to get the rep of the office player.

You can fall in love over morning coffee, indulge in a nooner on your lunch break, and be over the whole thing by quitting time. Off the clock, this may give you status as a hot property. On the clock, these antics will kill your career. Plus, your serial flirting will eventually seem skanky to those you subject to an endless stream of innuendo.

Since you aren't too great at being discreet, you might think the after-hours hookup with a coworker on the boss's carpet is such a good story that you can't help but spill it to a dozen of your office chums in the break room. Stop by the supply room on the way back to your office and pick up a couple of boxes to pack up your desk, because by the time the boss hears about your latest adventure, you and your charm will be history.

Yes, it's permissible to go out with a coworker in today's work environment. But it will never be kosher to use your workplace as your private dating service.

FROM FED UP TO FIRED UP

I'm a Gemini, so I change my mind every day.

NATALIE PORTMAN (JUNE 9)

You're articulate, curious, and open-minded. "What if" is one of your favorite phrases, and you'll often rework a project from a different slant to get the best possible result. Your colleagues can always rely on you to help them in a crisis.

You make yourself indispensable to your boss and coworkers by excelling in a high-pressure environment and by having an expansive imagination that results in ingenious solutions to almost any problem that pops up. Your challenge is to use your gift of gab in a positive way instead of blurting out the first thought that enters your mind.

Fight Fair

Your ability to think on your feet makes you good at office politics. When a feud erupts, you instinctively know how to play it safe. Smooth talker that you are, you can usually sidestep sensitive issues and have a knack for putting others on the spot while avoiding the hot seat yourself.

When you're irked at a colleague or vying for a top spot in the company, it's automatic for you to try to make him or her look bad. When you use rumor and innuendo or leak a confidence to deliberately harm someone's reputation, the only person you really discredit is yourself.

You are savvy enough on your own without resorting to underhanded tricks to win a promotion or snag a career-boosting assignment.

Know When to Quit

You tend to change jobs more often than some of the other signs. However, this isn't because you're a true job jumper.

One reason you walk out is because you toss up your hands in exasperation when your workload becomes a burden. Or you'll simply not show up again if you feel that you've been backed into a corner.

Truth is, you march into that corner all by yourself. You need to realize that you don't have to let anything in your life get to the point that you feel the only way out is to disappear. Like every Mutable sign, you hate confrontation. It's more comfortable for you to fall into verbal game playing than to sit down and try to hash out an issue.

One way you can combat the angst you feel when a problem arises is to take a conflict-resolution workshop. Armed with a few key phrases and basic guidelines, you'll be able to save face and salvage your job.

Ace an Interview

Your impressive résumé and glib charm gets your foot in the door. Then, along with Aries and Sagittarius, not knowing when to shut up can get you kicked back into the street.

The foremost thing for you to remember in an interview is not to ramble. There's a fine line between an informative, professional conversation and dumping useless minutiae that turns off a prospective employer. Although you like to present the big picture in hopes of making a good impression, try to stick to specifics. Focus on your qualifications and accomplishments that mesh with the job you seek.

Gemini anxiety can cause you to talk so fast that no one can understand half of what you're trying to say. Before the interview, practice talking slower. Watch yourself in the mirror or read aloud at a measured pace. Don't fuss with straightening your jacket or tie, or flail your hands around, either. Nervous gestures appear exaggerated in a one-on-one situation. Fiddling with your hair or fidgeting can send a signal to the interviewer that you might be too twitchy to have around.

While everyone pads their résumés a bit to make themselves look good, lying about who you know or what you've done in an interview leaves you wide open. It's like playing Russian roulette with your career. Stick to the facts, Gem. You have plenty of real virtues to impress a potential employer.

Gemini-Friendly Careers

Astrology lists media and communications at the top of your job qualification list. However, your silver tongue and stellar people skills will serve you well regardless of the career you choose. What you need in a career is freedom within guidelines to add your own perspective.

The following are several possibilities.

Writer

From investigative journalist to best-selling novelist, any career involving the written word is a natural for you.

Stand-Up Comic

Your wicked wit and amazing talent for impersonating anyone is a winning combination. Bonus: Here's where your caustic observations can make you rich and famous.

Teacher

Whether in grammar school, community education adult school, or college, helping others to discover their path in life is appealing. Plus your ability to make any subject interesting inspires your students to succeed.

Cartoonist

Your gift for satire and ability to present the truth from your own skewed perspective makes you a natural at creating sardonic, yet on-the-mark caricatures of life.

Salesperson

Whether you're selling haute couture to the fashionistas or heading up your own advertising firm, you possess a gift for convincing people that you have what they need.

CHAPTER FIVE

Cancer
June 21–July 22

Element:	Water
Quality:	Cardinal
Symbol:	The Crab
Ruler:	The Moon
Key word:	Industrious
Work-a-tude:	Don't rush me.

INSTANT INSIGHTS

I love sleep. My life tends to fall apart when I'm awake.

ERNEST HEMINGWAY (JULY 21)

Cancer, the Crab, is patient and kind. This *Feminine Cardinal Water* sign is also shrewd.

Because they're ruled by the ever-changing Moon, one of astrology's standard descriptions of these men and women is "moody." While that's true, never make the mistake of writing a Crab off as just another drama king or queen. Crabs are plenty tough, and as with all of the Cardinal signs, they feel that they were born to boss.

The Fourth House, where Cancer resides on the zodiac wheel, is all about home, past, present, and future. In traditional astrology it also represents mom, or the nurturing parent. Crabs think of their job as a home away from home and are inclined to treat coworkers more like extended family members than professional colleagues. Don't forget this. It's their biggest flaw and can be your biggest headache. Cancers are very perceptive and are understanding coworkers and bosses. Some also can't resist giving unwanted advice. In assigning themselves the role of Big Momma or Big Daddy, these Crabs often pry, and they rarely hesitate to manipulate and maneuver behind the scenes to get ahead.

All Water signs operate from the emotional perspective of feel first, act second. Fixed Water Scorpio rarely changes an opinion, and Mutable Water Pisces gets stuck trying to see every side. Cardinal Water Cancer has a you're-either-for-me-or-against-me mentality. Toss in a Feminine sensitivity driven by the cyclic Moon, and both sexes of this sign can have a permanent-PMS attitude toward life and work. Once you cross a Crab, you're forever on his or her hit list. Remember this before you decide to tell one to butt out of either your personal or professional life.

Fortunately, most Cancers are compassionate and attuned to other people's emotions. Your Crab friend, relative, or coworker is the first to sense when you're upset, and will reach out with a sympathetic ear and, usually, sound advice. He's dedicated to the people he cares about and will protect and defend the company he works for.

FAMOUS INDUSTRIOUS CANCERS

- Meryl Streep, the most Oscar-nominated actress in history— seventeen nominations, two wins (June 22)
- Michelle Kwan, the most decorated figure skater in U.S. history (July 7)
- John D. Rockefeller, America's first billionaire (July 8)

CANCER ON THE JOB

What I am good at is making people feel uncomfortable. I don't want to, but it always ends up happening.

JOSH HARTNETT (JULY 21)

In his futuristic novel *1984,* Cancer George Orwell coined the phrase "Big Brother is watching." Memorize it. The Crab is a born observer. He scrutinizes everyone and everything around him. This is because he's sizing up the company, the competition, and you.

These colleagues are industrious, inspiring, and usually devoted to creating long-term relationships in their careers. Supportive and loyal, your Cancer colleague will offer you her shoulder to cry on and usually dispenses surprisingly insightful advice.

Along with Libra, Cancer is a good negotiator. She can be counted on to help settle disputes and contribute to a peaceful atmosphere. A Crab is at her best when she's encouraging others to do their best.

All Cancers need to feel a sense of a family-like unit within the company, department, or their closest cubicle mates. Crack their protective shells by swapping vacation stories, showing pictures of your kids or cats, and asking to see pictures of their family.

Managing a Crab

Stay Close

Solving a last-minute crisis might be an Aquarian's cup of tea, but if you spring an eleventh-hour upheaval on your Cancer employee, he could go catatonic.

This doesn't mean that she can't handle an emergency; it's that her gut reaction is to withdraw from a crisis to assess the situation, then make a plan. Expecting a Cancer to make a snap decision is like waiting your turn to talk in a roomful of Sagittarians.

Many Crabs have a that's-the-way-we've-always-done-it outlook, but not necessarily because they're being arbitrary. Their fear of change makes them as prone to foot-dragging as either Taurus or Virgo. This results in a power struggle to get them to learn a new technology or accept even minor changes in department procedures. In these cases, you have to be the parent. If it's a new computer program, assign projects that force them to learn more than the basics. If a procedural change, send back everything that isn't in the new format. Pile on the praise as she makes progress to boost the Crab's self-confidence.

Luckily, most Crabs don't fall apart under pressure. However, being forewarned is forearmed. Being available and attentive when they need to voice their concerns reaps you a loyal, stick-by-your-side employee.

Keep Them Enthused

Extra perks might keep a Taurus plugging along without a raise for a while, but Cancer has a show-me-the-money attitude. He'll take the perks, but he also wants the dough. First, so that he can retire early and spend more time with his family. Second, because he has a fundamental fear of ending up alone and starving.

As does Taurus, your Cancer will function best with a clear understanding of how his merit increases work. Of course, if a true emergency arises, like a slump in sales or an across-the-board salary freeze, you can count on the loyal Crab to suck it up—for a while.

Since a Cancer is naturally money oriented and good with people, she'll excel when she can help both the company and the customer. Put her in a spot like accounts receivable. Her sympathy for others will result in a higher collection rate with minimum angst for your clients. She's as cost-conscious as any Capricorn, and in the accounting department she will find ingenious ways to shave extra dollars off the annual budget. Or let her run the customer service desk, where she instinctively knows how to soothe an upset patron. Positions that bring out her (and the male Crab, too) mothering instinct can produce amazing results for the bottom line.

Beware of Sneak Attacks

Because a Crab treats her job as an extension of her home, she's possessive of her responsibilities and work. She can also feel a sense of entitlement, whether or not it's justified.

I knew a Cancer supervisor who, after being promoted, was extremely irked that her boss didn't move her upstairs to the executive suite. It didn't matter to her that this was never the plan. She wanted a more prestigious corner office and made it her mission to maneuver to get it. Instead of concentrating on learning her new duties, she started a subtle, constant attack to discredit him whenever possible, including trying to blame him for several of her botched projects. Needless to say, this Crab's next promotion was to the open labor market.

While most Crabs aren't as underhanded, you can't always avoid this type of subtle subterfuge, even with a loyal one. Save yourself angst by following up important meetings with a written recap.

The prime rule to remember is that your Crab employee will diligently and happily do anything you ask—as long as you're headed in the same direction he is. Cardinal Cancer is an action sign. Even if it's two steps forward and one step back, a Crab never stops sidling toward his goal.

Surviving Boss Crab
Know What You're Dealing With

A Leo boss will take a risk on a get-rich-quick scheme. A Capricorn boss will weigh the odds but is also willing to go out on that money-making limb. The nest-egg-first Crab, however, is the least likely sign, including thrifty Taurus, to take a gamble.

While your Cancer boss is dedicated to making as much money as he can, he'd rather build up his fortune slowly, on his own terms, than engage in reckless speculation. Like every other Crab, he's driven by the fear of abject poverty.

Billionaire Richard Branson, a Cancer, has been quoted as saying, "I believe in a benevolent dictatorship, as long as I'm the dictator." So does your Cancer boss. He'll expect you to obey his rules. If you question him, he'll listen, but don't expect him or his policies to change.

Yes, she's moody. Yes, she can be crabby. However, Boss Crab can also be one of the most generous in the zodiac, as long as you're willing to work hard. If you can help her increase profits or get a bigger bonus by bringing in more sales, you can be sure that she'll share the wealth. That is, after she first pays her retirement fund, kids' college fund, and cautiously invests in a company expansion plan.

Be Considerate

Perceptive, wily, and tough in a clinch, Boss Crab can outmaneuver any other power player around.

What she won't do is take advantage of an underdog—either a weaker colleague or a struggling company. It's the mom thing. She might buy the struggling company, but it will be for a fair price and probably with the understanding that the current employees retain their jobs. She'll nurture her weak employee with extra guidance, and she'll expect the same from you. Whether you're dealing with a difficult manager in a different department or the moron across the room, be professional *and* kind.

This is another boss who has a hard time delegating, which can cause his desk to resemble that of an overeager Sagittarius. A Cancer hates to give up control of even day-to-day minutiae, and when he does, he's likely to stand over your shoulder to ensure you're doing it his way. Keep offering your help. Crabs appreciate persistence. Eventually, he'll hand over a project. It might be a small one to start, but if you treat him with the same patient consideration he shows to the slowest guy in your crew, you'll not only win Boss Crab's trust, but his loyalty. And you can take that to the bank.

CANCER WORDS TO LIVE BY

"You're only given a little spark of madness. You mustn't lose it."
—Robin Williams (July 22)

"You can't put a limit on anything. The more you dream, the farther you get."
—Michael Phelps (June 30)

Expect to be Micromanaged

A Capricorn boss keeps an eye on the time clock. A Libra boss can get tweak-happy with your presentation. A Cancer boss, however, can be the worst micromanager in the universe.

I knew a Cancer supervisor who spent more time telling one of her subordinates how to do a project than it took the woman to complete the task. It's an exasperating trait, but if you want to get along with Boss Cancer, you'll have to endure it at least some of the time. Depending on how enlightened she is, she'll either give you some control in prioritizing your workload or run the office like a second-grade teacher runs her classroom.

Fortunately, by the time most Cancer bosses make it up the corporate ladder they've learned to restrain this infuriating trait most of the time. For those other times, remember that this is also the boss who gave you an advance on your salary when the engine blew in your car and let you have extra time off when your grandparents came to visit.

Coping with a Cancer Coworker

The Crab is the zodiac's paradox. He can be moody one day, crazily funny the next, and all business the day after that. He's suspicious of other people's motives, yet he can be the first to encourage you to go back to school and be willing to work around your schedule. Once you learn how to break through his protective shell, you'll discover a kindhearted, witty, and wise friend.

Be Patient

If you think a Virgo can be routine-obsessed, asking your Cancer coworker to switch lunch hours with you could cause an emotional spinout. Crabs are creatures of habit. The best way for you to make friends with one is to respect this quirk.

Have an emergency and need help? That's a different story. She'll be the first to switch times and cover for you for while you're gone. She'll also most likely offer to drive you to the doctor, lawyer, or wherever you need to go.

As with Scorpio and Taurus, Cancers rarely rush into relationships on or off the clock. Knowing that can help you to avoid feeling rejected after the second time you ask her to go to lunch. Ask a third time. Chances are she'll decide that you're serious about being friends and not just being polite. Pacify her suspicious nature by not discussing work. It takes some effort to coax a Crab out of her shell; however, having this caring soul on your side is well worth the effort.

Keep Your Guard Up

Astrology paints Cancer as one of the martyrs of the zodiac. But behind every rotten Crab's seemingly sacrificial behavior is a scheming brain.

You don't have to argue with a bad Crab to become his target. Anything can set him off. It might be obvious jealously over your great working relationship with the rest of the crew or a concealed envy of your wardrobe or new office chair.

A spiteful Crab's capable of anything. He'll try to set you up by asking for your help on a project. Then after he screws it up, he'll tell a straight-faced lie that you left out an important component. He'll eavesdrop when you chat with other coworkers and spy on you while you're on a personal phone call, then tattle to the boss.

Cancer retreats, then attacks. It's a reliable pattern. Watch for a change in his behavior. If he suddenly warms up after being a jerk for a week, you can bet that before another week is up, he'll try to zing you.

A bad Crab rarely gives up the fight. As long as you're in close proximity, you can expect a snap now and then. Letting him have a verbal kick in the ass will shut him up for a while. The good news is that with time, the prodding and plotting will lessen.

CANCER CHEAP SHOTS

- Uses emotional blackmail
- Maneuvers behind your back
- Spies

Learn to Love Them

A thoughtful Cancer will remember your birthday with home-baked cupcakes or bring you a souvenir from her vacation. This tradition-loving sign clings to familiar faces and routines.

Although she can appear to be a loner, a Cancer hates solitude. Her reserve stems from a natural reticence to make the first move due to a fear of rejection. Bringing her a cup of coffee or sharing your morning doughnut will help to cement goodwill with the reclusive Crab.

Just as Cancer is full of hidden agendas, he's also full of hidden anxieties. Earn his trust by never betraying a secret, even a small one. Like Scorpio and Libra, if a Cancer likes you, he'll subject you to a series of little tests to determine whether it's safe for him to trust you. Once he does, you'll have an office pal you can rely on no matter what.

IF YOU ARE A CANCER

Never confuse movement with action.
NELSON MANDELA (JULY 18)

You can tell when someone is frustrated or overwhelmed and you're always ready to offer assistance or a morale boost. There isn't a job you can't handle or a dilemma you can't solve. You'll stick with a job until it's finished, and your colleagues can count on you when they need advice.

How then can you push your career from ordinary to exceptional?

Get in Gear

Being a Cardinal sign, you'll always take action—eventually. But you can be so slow that by the time you decide to make a move, opportunity is lost.

By taking one more class, one more seminar, or getting one more degree under your belt, you may tell yourself that you're readying for a big career change. In reality, your be-prepared belief system is based on fear of the unknown. But you have to take risks if you want to succeed.

Even if you don't intend to quit your current job, it won't hurt to see what's out there. Polish your résumé and send it out. Go on interviews. Call them practice runs if you want. You don't have to take a job if it's offered. However, the more you look around, the less anxious you'll be about making a change when you find a better position.

Yes, you're cautious. But we all know there's no such thing as a sure thing, except that in today's competitive market, hesitating is a sure way to kill your career. You're more than capable of snagging any job you want, so don't waste either your time or your life settling for less than you can achieve.

Misery is Optional

Insightful Crab Harrison Ford said, "Being happy is something you have to learn." While this is good advice for every sign, it's crucial for you because you can become a slave to your ever-changing moods. Although you might get away with having revolving-door emotions in your private life, failing to curb them in your professional life could move you so far down the corporate ladder that you end up in a closet-size office in the basement.

Along with Aries, you must learn to pick your battles. If you complain every time you feel you've been slighted, you'll not only be in the boss's office several times a day, you'll never be taken seriously when a real issue arises.

It's easy to avoid the office hypocrite who gossips behind everyone's back. Putting up with a hard-nosed higher-up can be aggravating, but it doesn't have to be demoralizing. Practice your poker face when she's being critical and smile when she acts halfway decent. You don't have many options if she's in a power position. So unless it's a serious breach of policy or something illegal, playing office politics will help you in the long run.

Here's a thought. As you're a self-motivating sign who's determined to move up, play the game until *you're* the boss—then fire the bitch.

TIPS FOR SUCCESS

- Take a risk
- Curb your touchy side
- Learn to let go

Cut the Puppet Strings

Another way you shoot yourself in the foot is by trying to manipulate your environment. Although you're good at helping your coworkers work out compromises, you can be as obtuse as Taurus when it comes to readjusting your own point of view. Learn to let go of the small stuff first. Does it really matter whether you take your break at 9:45 or 10:00?

Instead of speaking up in a staff meeting or voicing a concern directly to the person you should, you move from coworker to coworker attempting to convince each one to take your side. To your office mates, your under-the-table negotiations come across as underhanded tricks to get your way.

You're one of the assertive signs, but your Feminine, Moon-ruled soul can assert itself in a negative way. That's because you can be as timid as a real crab. You know how it zigs and zags across the sand, making headway but moving from rock to rock for safety? That's the way your emotions work. Taking the direct approach can be as frightening to you as scuttling out in the open is to that crab on the beach.

If you want to move up, compromise is essential. So is understanding that confrontation doesn't automatically mean conflict. With practice, you can learn to speak up instead of maneuvering behind the scenes. As smart as you are, you'll soon have your opponent eating out of your hand.

FROM FED UP TO FIRED UP

I always look for a challenge and something that's different.

TOM CRUISE (JULY 3)

You're warm, compassionate, and supportive. Like Pisces, you have an intuitive people radar that's seldom wrong. You're persevering, patient, and always have a plan for moving ahead. Your challenge is to learn how to cope with the unexpected without either falling apart or suffering a major setback.

Nurture Yourself

One of your best traits is helping others succeed. So why is it that you're often the last person to benefit from your inspiration and encouragement?

Instead of worrying about the talents you think you lack, make a list of the ones you have. Keep them handy for your rainy-day states of mind. Stay on the cutting edge of your career with classes and networking. Learning something new is great for your self-esteem.

Every sign needs R&R, but it's vital to your ability to cope with job stress. Schedule time for a weekly massage or pedicure, or walk in the park. Join your office chums for happy hour now and then. Getting to know your cubicle mates off the clock can boost your self-confidence and help them see your fun-loving side. It won't kill your family to cook their own dinner once a month. Stressing out from heaping too much pressure on yourself can kill your career.

Know When to Quit

Of the four Cardinal signs, you're the most reluctant to leave a job, even when you know that you should. That's because your job also becomes your security blanket.

Your out-of-the-frying-pan-into-the-fire fear can keep you in an unfavorable situation far too long. When that happens, you become one miserable Crab who keeps to herself and counts the hours until quitting time each day. If this happens to you, it's way past time to get out.

Cold calling prospective employers can be an obstacle because you don't like being subjected to the vetting process of a Human Resource department. A good option for you is to find a highly regarded recruitment firm. Establishing a relationship with your own personal job shopper reduces your angst in dealing with a series of strangers.

You're full of fears, most of which are head trips you subject yourself to out of insecurity. In reality, you're one tough Crab who can conquer any obstacle. Once you believe this about yourself, nothing can stop you. Going stale in a safe but nowhere job might get you a pension at retirement, but you have it in you to catch your dream, so don't be afraid to shoot for the Moon.

Ace an Interview

Your professional demeanor and instinct for knowing what an interviewer wants to hear puts you on the leading candidates list. Then a couple of your unconscious traits can get you shoved to the bottom of the reject pile.

Got a photo album? Study your facial expressions in various candid photos. You might be surprised to see that many times you look as if you're frowning, or worried, even though that wasn't what you felt when the picture was snapped. The habit you have of furrowing your brow or wrinkling your nose makes you look as if you're either hiding something or condescending, which immediately turns off anyone you're trying to impress.

When you're nervous, you tend to sink back into the chair and/or slouch. It's your way of withdrawing from an anxiety-provoking situation. Be aware of your posture and sit up, keep your head up, and smile.

It's both smart and expected to have questions about the company or the position you're applying for. However, your tendency to interview the interviewer can come across as an interrogation, making her feel that you're too fussy to risk hiring.

You light up when you smile and have a quiet charm that can win over the most hardened interviewer. Consciously allow that side of your personality out. You can get almost any job you apply for, Crab cake, if you get out of your own way.

Cancer-Friendly Careers

While most astrology books suggest professions such as social worker or therapist, your gift for creating harmony and ability to inspire others can bring success in any career you choose.

What you need is to work at your own pace within a safety net of dependable colleagues in a profession that gives you the freedom to control your environment while giving you as much stability as possible.

The following are several career possibilities.

Wedding Planner

Your flair for meticulous planning, intuiting what people want, and creating an elegant affair, even on a tight budget, keeps your calendar booked solid.

Obstetrician or Family Practice Physician

Whether you're helping bring a baby into the world or writing out a healthy-lifestyle plan for a retiree, your patients become part of your extended family. Bonus: You get to dispense all the motherly advice you want.

History Teacher or Museum Curator

Whether as a teacher inspiring your students to study ancient cultures or as a curator preserving antiquities, you find working with ideas and items from the past appealing.

Bodyguard

Protecting the privacy of your client is instinctive. Plus your loyalty and confidentiality reaps the job security you crave.

Bed-and-Breakfast Owner

Turning your talent for TLC into making a home away from home for tired vacationers who need pampering could make you rich.

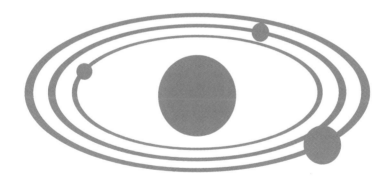

CHAPTER SIX

Leo
July 23–August 22

Element:	Fire
Quality:	Fixed
Symbol:	The Lion
Ruler:	The Sun
Key word:	Responsible
Work-a-tude:	Listen to me.

INSTANT INSIGHTS

Anything worth doing is worth overdoing.

MICK JAGGER (JULY 26)

From a lion prowling the jungle to the cat purring in your lap, every feline is playful, protective, and predatory—including the human version. He won't hesitate to plunge into a crisis to rescue a friend, relative, or coworker. He also won't hesitate to confront anyone who stands between him and something he wants.

Masculine Fixed Fire Leo is ruled by the Sun. Some astrological traits attributed to a Lion include generous, cheerful, and straightforward. Egotistical, high-maintenance, and pushy also describe people born under this sign. This exuberant character might jump in the middle of the dance floor at a party, but unlike Aries, he rarely stoops to bratty behavior to get noticed. He doesn't have to. If you know a Leo, you know that even a quiet one has a potent personality.

Leo lives in the zodiac's Fifth House of creativity, romance, and children. This is also the crib of indulgence and recreation. Every Lion has a childlike enthusiasm for fun and is as willing to play hooky as he is to burn the midnight oil. He can be as convincing as any Gemini and twice as energetic as a Sagittarius. He'll make his latest scheme sound so brilliant and fail-safe that he rounds up investors in a heartbeat. This talent for getting other people fired up often results in fabulous business deals—and just as fabulous failures.

Astrology advises that all Fixed signs are stubborn. Watery Scorpio has fixed emotions: She either likes something or she doesn't. Earthy Taurus has a fixed outlook on life—don't make changes. Airy Aquarius has fixed ideas: "I know I'm right." However, Leo's fixed fire burns steady. Just as the Sun is the center of our universe, a Lion thrives on being the center of her world. The problem with this concept is the omission of one important word—responsibility. Leo feels that she's responsible for keeping her world productive, and the only way she can do that is if she runs the show. It's a big job.

FAMOUS LEADING LIONS

- Barack Obama, first black president of the United States (August 4)
- Steve Case, cofounder of AOL online (August 21)
- Gene Roddenberry, creator of *Star Trek* (August 19)

LEO ON THE JOB

I have my little list of those that treated me unfairly.

JENNIFER LOPEZ (JULY 24)

Whether he's your team leader, the guy washing your car, or your friendly banker, the Lion is a cheerful people magnet. Although a Leo can be as tradition-loving as any Taurus, he's also one of the zodiac's risk takers. He's attracted to power and prestige, and he isn't afraid to lay either his money or his reputation on the line to get ahead.

Sun-ruled Leo is the most prideful sign in the universe. This is both the source of her ability to do a great job and her biggest flaw. Always treat this colleague with the same respect that you'd give a real lion if you met one strolling down the street. Don't act afraid, but don't ask for trouble, either. As with all Fixed signs, she has a long memory. If you've wounded her pride, she's capable of pouncing on you when you least expect it.

He'll think he's right most of the time and give orders even if he's not the boss. But his sunny outlook makes the most boring job more fun, and you can trust the Lion to stick with you when times are rough.

Managing a Lion
Give Them Atta-Boys

Pat an egotistical Lion's head? That sounds crazy, right? Here's a secret. A Lion's ego act is rooted in an inner fear that he or she won't measure up. *Confidence* and *courage* are traits that get confused when referring to Leos. Lions act with courage even when they don't feel very self-confident.

Being too proud to ask for help, admit a mistake, or apologize has earned Leo the reputation of being arrogant, but the real reason for this overblown behavior is that they can be very self-conscious. Lions are natural gamblers who are great at bluffing. Many times, the wilder he acts, the less sure of himself he is.

Everyone needs to feel appreciated, but Lions crave acknowledgement of their effort. The in-your-face type will demand it. The quiet type will expect it without having to ask. Whichever one you work with, stroke his ego with a well-meant compliment. You don't have to gush, as with a Libra. A simple "great job" will do. Giving your Lion a show of approval, especially in front of his peers, earns both his loyalty and his dedication to work even harder.

Keep Them Enthused

As do we all, Lions value the usual raises, a bonus when appropriate, and a perk now and then. A Lion's main motivation is recognition. One of the fastest ways to make your Leo employee happy is to give her a title and put her in a visible spot. Anything that starts with coordinator, director, head, or lead is a good start. Whether she's greeting patrons at a five-star restaurant or scheduling appointments at the spa, to her, a title separates her from the average worker bee—even if she is one.

No matter what his duties are, he's full of ideas that cross every level of the company. Let him explain his advertising strategy or present his plan for rotating work tasks to keep the staff educated and motivated. Whether he's selling tires or million-dollar real estate, every Leo has a natural flair for knowing what customers want and how to keep them happy. Put this attention-loving sign in the public eye, and he'll thrive. So will business.

Don't Relax the Reins

Inside the most diligent Leo is a lazy cat who would love to sleep all day and prowl all night. Let up the pace, and the Lion can slack off faster than a Libra punches the time clock at quitting time.

This isn't the same as monitoring Pisces's or Gemini's progress with frequent minideadlines. Procrastination isn't an issue with Leo. It's about providing a steady workflow that prevents him from turning the workplace into his private social club. This cat can become the king of joke e-mails, or spend more time making the rounds of other departments to talk to his friends than sitting at his desk.

Stick her in a hot spot where she puts out fires. Even if she bitches that she's overworked, she likes being the person everyone else relies on for help. To the Lion, satisfied customers equal a happy audience. As a team leader, her straightforward and generous nature earns her colleagues' respect. She's good at details and will turn in a project as perfect as any

Virgo can, in less time. Keep your Leo busy, preferably in direct contact with other people, and watch her become a star performer.

Surviving Boss Lion
Know What You're Dealing With

Although Boss Lion can be the most high-maintenance boss in the zodiac, he's also charismatic and patient. That is, when he's not roaring.

Every Fire sign has a hard time containing its emotions. Leo doesn't even try. A headstrong Lion in a snit can make the most obnoxious Aries look like a rank amateur. He'll argue. He'll fire off memos. He might even shout. Don't worry. Although he might lose his temper more often than Boss Archer, he gets over his tantrums almost as quickly. Unless you've really screwed up, you can be confident that the Lion won't aim his anger at you. Even if he should, as long as you don't lie to him, this boss is all about giving second chances.

Whether he's a self-employed contractor or the department head of an insurance company, every Leo boss craves admiration. A Capricorn boss might smile if you offer a compliment. A Scorpio boss might wonder what you're after. But Boss Lion needs to hear that he's a great boss or be asked for his help with a problem. In fact, he expects it.

Leo rock star Madonna has been quoted as saying, "I'd like to see the Pope wearing my T-shirt." Remember that your boss feels the same way—he wants everyone to be a fan, whether or not they're in the same line of work.

Working for a Leo is similar to being the concierge at a five-star hotel: You never know who's going to walk through the door. One day he could be in low-key mode, entertaining a buddy who's in town for the weekend. The next day, he'll show up in his best suit ready to negotiate a megabucks deal with a group of power brokers. You need to be as comfortable switching gears as he is.

Stay on Your Toes

Boss Leo likes being a role model and is willing to take extra time to ensure that you know your job. Once you learn it, he'll expect nothing less than 100 percent from you at all times.

As does Taurus, your Leo boss believes in consistent output. The difference is that Boss Lion expects you to consistently operate in high gear. He does. He can multitask as well as any Gemini. However, he feels that he has more important things to do than to wrestle everyday minutiae. That's your job. Help him to stay on top of his projects and turn your work in ahead of time whenever you can, and he'll think you're a genius he can't do without.

Astrology describes the Fixed signs as *unchanging* or *slow to change.* Memorize this, because Boss Lion will always get his way. The good news? This boss is just as loyal to you as he expects you to be to him. That's another thing he won't change.

Expect Advice—Lots of It

Most bosses are concerned about their employees' personal lives to a certain extent. However, Boss Lion can be as snoopy as Aries and as free with advice as Gemini.

Boss Lion is as curious as a house cat and as patient. If she has the slightest suspicion that your boyfriend is being a jerk, or you're searching for a new house, or babysitter, or vehicle, she's compelled to offer suggestions, referrals, and the name of her sports car salesman. Don't mistake her interest for Cancer's attempt to turn the office into an extension of her home. Leo doesn't want to add you to her list of relatives; her motive is based on the responsibility she feels for everything within her world.

Another area that you might get well-meant but pushy counsel is about your style. While neatness counts with every boss, image is everything to a Leo. They're famous for maxing out a credit card to keep up appearances. Boss Lion sees you as an extension of himself. Don't think you have to ditch your wardrobe, however; keeping your look updated with a couple of inexpensive pieces in this year's style is all it takes.

Yes, it's annoying to have a boss who might try to push her way into your personal life. But it's also reassuring to realize that you have a boss who *is* interested in your life and will try to help you make it better.

LEO WORDS TO LIVE BY

"People who never get carried away, should be."
—Malcolm Forbes (August 19)

"It's only when you hitch your wagon to something larger than yourself that you realize your true potential."
—Barack Obama (August 4)

Coping with a Leo Coworker

Whether he's a bouncy Lion who keeps you laughing or a quiet cat who gets attention by being the best at what he does, all Leos are usually upbeat and enthusiastic. This coworker won't hesitate to help out when you're overloaded or party with you after work. High-spirited Leos keep the office humming with energy.

Be Assertive

There's a misconception that all Leos are scene-stealing prima donnas who will do anything to be the center of attention. That said, you can count on him to be a nuisance at least part of the time. Whether he's roaring about something that he thinks is unfair or he wants you to drop everything and listen to his latest brainstorm, don't hesitate to ask him to save it until break time. Don't be nasty, just matter-of-fact. A Lion respects honesty and understands a strong work ethic. When you refuse to let him monopolize your time at his convenience, he'll respect your attitude, and you'll win an ally.

Keep Your Guard Up

While a Leo won't hesitate to go after what she wants, most do it with the same dogged determination of a Capricorn. They set goals and work toward them, letting little get in their way.

Compete with a ruthless Lion and be prepared for a jungle fight. Unlike an Aries, who'll tell you she's after the same project, or a Cancer, who'll sneak behind your back, a bad Lion will pounce in public. She'll confront you at every opportunity, and her only aim will be to make you look stupid, especially if she can stage it so that the boss is around.

The best way to combat this behavior is to keep your head. If you get embarrassed or start stammering, you'll prove that she's right. Remember that Lions are risk takers. She'll gamble that she can catch you off guard and make you look bad. Be prepared, and you'll stop her in her tracks.

LEO CHEAP SHOTS

- Discredits you in front of others
- Interrupts and expects your attention
- Snoops in your personal life

Learn to Love Them

I once worked with three Leos, all in the same department. One was quiet, one was brash, and one was very prideful. When they worked, they worked hard. When they stopped to play, no one worked. It was entertaining, exasperating, and wild.

Asking a Leo's advice when a project hits a snag makes him feel useful and important. Listening to him when he's fuming earns his confidence. Offer advice if you want; however, don't get offended if he ignores it. Leo is the least likely sign to follow anyone else's guidance.

Most of the time, you can't help but like a playful, exuberant Lion. Even when he's trying to tell you how to do your job, his motive is usually to be helpful. He'll appreciate your help, too. Offer it when you see he's jamming to keep up.

Few signs are as good at inspiring you to believe in yourself and cheering you on when you go after a dream. Return that support, and you'll not only have a loyal coworker, you'll make a phenomenal friend.

IF YOU ARE A LEO

I'm always described as "cocksure" or "with a swagger," and that bears no resemblance to who I feel like inside. I feel plagued by insecurity.

BEN AFFLECK (AUGUST 15)

You're ambitious, independent, and kindhearted. There isn't a boss you can't impress or a coworker you can't turn into a friend. You'll pitch in wherever you're needed and work longer and harder than anyone else to get the job done, and your team spirit is often the glue that keeps your coworkers on track.

So how can you take your career from average to astounding?

Remember Who the Real Boss Is

You have a powerful personality and like to have an insider's view of what goes on at your job. Where you get into trouble is when you try to get too chummy with the boss in hopes that you'll get on the fast track, and when you push your ideas onto your coworkers without running them by the boss for approval. The first scenario makes you look like a major suck-up, and the second can put you on the fast track to the unemployment line. You need to respect the chain of command if you want to be taken seriously.

That doesn't mean that you shouldn't try to promote yourself (as if anyone could stop you!), but do it in a professional way. If the boss turns down one of your ideas, ask for suggestions on how it can be improved. Ask to form a team to look into a process that you think could function more effectively.

Making your boss an ally by respecting her position and authority is smart. Plus, you'll get the reputation as a team player who's interested in benefiting the company, not only yourself.

Dismount Your High Horse

Despite your sunny disposition and generous nature, you can be as determined to convince others you are right as an Aquarius ranting about the latest conspiracy theory.

I knew a Leo who started many conversations with, "If you do what I tell you . . ." He thought he was being helpful. Everyone else thought he was an overbearing bore. Your suggestions are usually levelheaded and your motives well intended. It's how you present them that can irk your colleagues. Instead of making a statement, ask a question: "Do you think it might work this way?" "Would you mind if I took a look?" Use your charisma to get your point across, then let it go. Not everyone is receptive to new ideas, and some will be suspicious of your motives. In fact, you should understand that, as yours is one of the worst signs in the zodiac about taking anyone else's advice.

TIPS FOR SUCCESS

- Don't step on the boss's toes
- Rein in your ego
- Control your urge to prowl on company time

Don't Overexercise Your Flirt Muscles

You love to push boundaries. Flirting comes as naturally to you as fantasizing does to a Pisces. When you're on the prowl, few can resist your charms. Blend all of these factors, and anyone would have a recipe for on-the-job romantic mayhem.

Add your need for attention, plus the perception that you can get away with anything, and you've just whipped up a formula for disaster. Along with Aries, Gemini, and Sagittarius, you're not opposed to heading for the supply room for a quickie on your break or staying after hours for a tryst in the boss's office.

I knew a Leo who pulled that trick once. He very much disliked his boss and felt trapped because, although he liked the company, he had no options for transfer at that time. So in his charismatic Lion way, he talked his girlfriend into doing the deed on top of the boss's desk. Although he admitted afterward that it was a stupid stunt, he couldn't help smiling to himself each time he walked by his boss's open door.

I knew another Leo who wasn't so lucky. She was cute, bouncy, and went through the personnel roster of single cuties with the same dedication as a Taurus chomping through a five-course meal. Unfortunately, she became the target of the company grapevine and left a promising job with her Lion self-esteem crushed.

As ambitious as you are, and with a world full of willing lovers outside of the workplace, never take the risk of ruining your career by letting your vanity overrule your common sense.

FROM FED UP TO FIRED UP

Nothing big ever came of being small.
BILL CLINTON (AUGUST 19)

You are independent, assertive, and very aware of what's going on around you.

You fight for what you want and aren't afraid to stand up for yourself. You'll also fight for your friends and coworkers, and stand up for an underdog. Your challenge is to view the advice you get from others as help that can propel you forward faster instead of an insult to your Lion's ego.

Share the Praise

Your Fixed soul resists change unless you initiate it. Your ego is tied up with gaining attention by saving the day or inspiring others—the hero habit. Plus, you crave the kudos that fixing the project, proposal, or customer complaint brings you. This is why your first instinct is to balk when anyone offers you a suggestion on how to do things better, and you can get jealous when a coworker gets more attention than you do. You mistakenly believe that accepting help or sharing the spotlight makes you look weak or, worse to you, average.

You're known as a team player. In reality, you either want to lead the team or be its star. The two quickest ways to win over your colleagues are to be liberal with sharing the credit and kudos, and to ask their opinions. Once you practice this approach, you'll learn that, contrary to making you less influential, it actually earns you more respect and, consequently, more power.

Know When to Quit

Because you're a Fixed sign, you aren't a true job jumper. Usually, one of two things happens that can harm your career: You turn into a chronic complainer who bitches about everything but won't take action, or you blow small issues way out of proportion and walk out in a huff. Either way, you lose.

Former president Bill Clinton said, "Sometimes I feel like the fire hydrant looking at a pack of dogs." If you feel like this, it might be time to dust off your résumé. On the other hand, you could be exaggerating the issue.

Stop and think before you type up your resignation letter. Are you leaving for a better position and not because your pride's been wounded? If you like your job, is there a way you can work around whatever's standing in your way? Once you can tell the difference between when you're being held back and when you're overreacting, you'll go further and faster than anyone else in the universe.

Ace an Interview

Your confident handshake and attractive appearance make an instant good impression on any interviewer. Letting your ego run away with your mouth can just as instantly send you to the reject pile.

The interviewer might be in awe of your credentials. However, if you start to brag or act as if he should be bowled over, he'll think that you're too arrogant to take a chance on. Your résumé speaks for itself, so use restraint when discussing your qualifications.

When nervous, Taurus mumbles, Gemini blathers, and you shout. An Aries can also talk loud, but when you have the jitters, it often agitates the entertainer side of your character, and you're in danger of acting like a knee-slapping dimwit. As looking bad in front of others can be one of your worst fears, keep that in mind to keep yourself on track.

You have an inner strength that gets you through anything. Plus, your charismatic personality can win over anyone. You don't need to puff yourself up with false pride, because you're already an impressive character.

Leo-Friendly Careers

Astrology lists you as one of the true people persons of the universe. While not every Lion wants to be in the public eye, the majority of you need to be involved with other people in some way to feel successful. Where you'll thrive is in a profession that allows you to take control so that you have the freedom to explore your ideas and dreams without restraint.

The following are some Lion-size suggestions.

Entertainer

Actor, dancer, rock star, or hometown celebrity—all can appeal to your love of being in the spotlight and adored by everyone around.

Politician

Whether you're running for class president or have your eye on the White House, your charisma and the natural ease with which you can convince people that you have all the answers makes you everyone's ideal candidate.

Speculator

Flipping houses, playing the market, or investing in your own business appeals to the gambler in your soul. Due to your instinct for sniffing out great deals, you usually win.

Personal Trainer

Helping your clients improve both their health and self-image satisfies your desire to help others. Bonus: You get to show off your hot body.

Manager

Whether managing the career of a public figure, a chain of jewelry shops, or the neighborhood bistro, your lead-by-example style and enthusiasm for helping others achieve personal success is a win-win formula.

CHAPTER SEVEN

Virgo

August 23–September 22

Element:	Earth
Quality:	Mutable
Symbol:	The Virgin
Ruler:	Mercury
Key word:	Methodical
Work-a-tude:	Do it right the first time.

INSTANT INSIGHTS

I get nervous when I don't get nervous.

BEYONCÉ KNOWLES (SEPTEMBER 4)

Ever wonder why your Virgo coworker, friend, or relative can turn the simplest task into a brain-deadening project? One reason is that this sign resides in the Sixth House of work and health on the astrological wheel. From grocery shopping to balancing the budget, Virgos tackle every project with the same dedication to details that they tackle their job.

Feminine Mutable Earth Virgo is ruled by Mercury, the god of information. Although Mercury also rules airy Gemini, in earthy Virgo, Mercury's winged feet are kept securely on the ground. This results in some contradictory behavior traits. Despite being Mutable (flexible), a Virgo can be as reluctant to change his viewpoint as any Fixed sign. Mutable Air

Gemini will make compromises. Mutable Water Pisces will go along with the crowd. Virgo, however, appears to negotiate. In reality, getting a Virgin to change his mind can be as impossible as getting a Scorpio to spill a family secret. This isn't egotistical, as a Leo can get. Many Virgos operate from feelings of inferiority, and to them, taking the long way to accomplish a project or personal goal ensures they have covered all the bases.

Virgos have the astrological reputation for being the zodiac's perfectionist, but it's not true perfection they seek, it's Virgo-order. Your Virgo colleague can be uncompromising about the way he handles his life or work. Virgo believes in the precision of a well-run job site, consistent schedule, and a backup plan for everything. The caveat is that this "*be prepared*" attitude can go insanely out of whack.

Because of the Sixth House health connection, a Virgo's mental and physical health is directly related to her job stress level. Even more than a Cancer, the Virgin can literally make herself ill over a work-related crisis. That's why these natives need to take regular breaks, not eat lunch at their desks, and schedule frequent weekend getaways to relax.

Another contradiction with Virgo is that, unlike the other Mutable signs of Gemini, Sagittarius, and Pisces, a Virgin does not make friends easily. Even though they are pleasant to be around and friendly, they can be as tight-lipped about sharing even mundane personal facts as any Scorpio.

Most Virgos want to do their jobs quietly, efficiently, and with as little fanfare as possible. They don't strive for center stage or to know all the grapevine gossip. Virgos want to be productive and feel useful.

FAMOUS UNCOMPROMISING VIRGOS

- Tim Burton, director of Batman and many other hit movies (August 25)
- Warren Buffet, billionaire investor and humanitarian (August 30)
- Faith Hill, country/pop crossover singer and five-time Grammy winner (September 21)

VIRGO ON THE JOB

Rule Number 1: Never lose money. Rule Number 2: Never forget rule Number 1.

WARREN BUFFET (AUGUST 30)

The good news about having a Virgo work buddy is that you can count on him to do the same thing, in the same way, at the same time, every time. That's also the bad news.

Think that because Virgo's usually referred to as the sign of organization this means they are time-savers? Not true. This native can get so stuck in the details that he will actually double the time it takes to do a job. Plus, he'll make himself sick when the pressure's on and everyone else angry by his constant tweaking.

If he's dealing with the public, it's best not to stick a Virgo in a hot spot. He'll worry more than a Capricorn fearing a stock market slide. He might act calm, cool, and collected, but inside, your average Virgin is full of nervous anxiety. Most Virgos do best in a quiet, routine-oriented position.

Being friendly but not pushy and casually sharing tidbits about your personal life will gradually break through a Virgo's reserve. Once you do, you'll discover a kindhearted, chatty office pal whom you can turn to when you need help.

Managing a Virgin
Get the Rules Straight

Astrology defines a Virgo as an excellent critic. The truth is that he is an absolutely *compulsive* critic. It is said that music legend Ray Charles, a Virgo, recorded all four tracks of his blues hit "I Believe To My Soul" after sending his backup group, the Raelettes, home for not producing the quality he wanted.

Charles's dedication to doing it his way did produce a hit record, but unless you want the annual report to become a three-volume missive of minutiae, give your Virgo specifics. That includes a deadline. Virgos can procrastinate as bad as any Pisces. However, it's because they tweak a project to death versus delay getting started as the Fish will.

Asking a Virgo for periodic progress reports take some finesse. Your Virgo has a huge defense mechanism that kicks in anytime you question her about any aspect of her job. This is because of a basic lack of confidence. She'll automatically assume that, if you're checking up on her, she must be doing something wrong. Set a schedule at the same time you hand over the project, then leave her alone. The Virgin can be counted on to hand in progress reports on time, and you'll earn her loyalty for trusting her to do a good job.

Put your Virgin in a spot where he can monitor the work of others. Let him proof reports or spot-check product quality. His blend of a Mercury-ruled intellect and practical Earth character ensures that errors will drop and production will increase.

Keep Them Enthused

A Virgo might work at a slow pace, but his mind is always in high gear. He's great at solving multipart problems and handling projects that have tons of factors to consider. Let your Virgo plan and supervise an office move or be responsible for the endless details of starting up a new department. He'll handle everything from ordering furniture, computers, and supplies to organizing staff training schedules. Or, put him in a think tank where his analytical mind can save the company money when he spots the flaws in a new plan before it gets to the design stage.

Money motivates everyone to a certain degree, but Virgos need respect and appreciation to really flourish. She might laugh off your praise or make a self-deprecating remark, but don't let that stop you. Telling her she's done well bolsters this sign's sometimes lack of self-esteem.

Let your Virgo be the problem solver and organizer you count on to keep your workplace running, and you'll soon have a well-oiled, highly productive money-making organization.

Head Off the Hypochondriac

A Virgin under stress can talk herself into anything from flulike symptoms to the latest designer disease. Whether you're having a surprise audit or it's the peak of busy season in a retail shop, your Virgo, similar to Cancer, can disappear into Sick-Time Land at the worst possible moment. A signal of an impending meltdown is when she complains more than usual. She's overworked. How do you expect her to handle everything alone?

This is when you step in to offer help. Ask direct questions. Virgo can be as obtuse as Taurus and as evasive as Pisces. If he's complaining about shouldering more than his share of the load, ask him what would help. Virgos hate to admit they can't handle a job. Chances are, he won't have a good answer.

What he needs is reassurance. Tell him he's doing a great job and how much you appreciate his hard work. Say that you don't know how you'd get along without him and that as soon as the rush is over, he deserves a long weekend to relax.

Virgos respond to a quiet voice and friendly smile. Talk to yours in a nonthreatening way, and you'll soothe her nerves and save your own sanity.

Surviving Boss Virgin
Know What You're Dealing With

The great thing about a Virgo boss is that she won't hesitate to help you with whatever you need to do your job. She'll answer your questions and see that you get properly trained. In fact, she'll probably hand you a procedure manual with detailed instructions.

The not-so-great thing about Boss Virgo is that, second only to a Cancer, she's the world's greatest micromanager. "Nobody does it better" is her motto, and she'll make it her mission to prove it, even if it kills you both.

The reason for his microscopic management style is that, like Pisces, most Virgos are not truly comfortable being the head of anything. All will suffer bouts of crankiness even if they are managing six employees at the family-owned pizzeria. Don't misunderstand—they can produce amazing profits and create a loyal staff. But they all feel a gigantic burden when propelled to the head office.

Despite the daily criticism and occasional nervous outburst, Boss Virgo is one of the kindest bosses in the zodiac. He's honest. He'll help you prioritize when your inbox overflows, and he won't arbitrarily change the rules or spring any wild surprises on you. That alone is worth hearing him grumble now and then.

Stay on Top of Things

Boss Virgo might not walk in the office exactly at the same time every day, but you should. Plus, turn your work in on time, take your lunch and breaks at the same time each day, and don't clock out a minute before quitting time.

This boss appreciates order. Although his desk might look like he switched offices with the Sagittarius down the hall, he'll have his own weird system for knowing where to find anything in the chaos. So don't assume that he's too scattered to notice the piles on your desk or the fact that you spent an hour e-mailing your pals. He will. As does Taurus, Boss Virgo can get touchy when you waste time on his dime.

If you're his administrative assistant, make sure your letters and reports are typo-free and centered on the page. If you're his mechanic, be sure you show him the parts you replaced on his car and explain why it was necessary.

Boss Virgo wants both his life and his job to run like clockwork. If you keep the filing caught up, the supply cabinet well stocked, and his calendar perfectly updated, he'll know that he can't get along without you.

VIRGO WORDS TO LIVE BY

"Don't be against things so much as for things."
—Colonel Harlan Sanders (September 9)

"I'm not going to start planning anything. My life is way better than anybody could have planned it."
—Rachael Ray (August 25)

Learn to Tune Out

A Capricorn boss will put up a brave front even if the roof's caving in. A Taurus boss will expect you to follow his instructions no matter what. But the more pressure a Virgo boss feels, the more she'll nag you to work harder, longer, and faster. If it's any consolation, she's a boss who expects even more from herself. But if there's a fire to put out and you're stuck with the job, you'll wish you had a set of earplugs.

I once worked with three other people in a tiny office. Our new manager was a nail-biting Virgo guy who drove himself, and us, crazy with periodic harangues over everything from minor work-related issues to the way the plant service maintained the philodendron. After a while we realized that his eruptions always coincided with an unexpected upheaval. The rest of the time he was witty, chatty, and treated us more as friends than subordinates. We realized that his outbursts were never aimed directly at anyone but were a general stress-related fussiness.

When your Virgo boss goes off on a tangent, be kind. Ask how you can help, or offer to stay late before she has to ask. She might not take you up on it, but you'll earn both her gratitude and her loyalty.

Coping with a Virgo Coworker

The quickest way to make friends with a Virgo colleague is to understand that she's a creature of habit. Interrupting her train of thought or asking her to switch lunch hours can throw her off kilter for the rest of the day. This coworker will be as considerate of your space and routine as she expects you to be of hers. Respect her boundaries, and you'll soon discover the kind, funny, friendly side of your Virgo work buddy.

Be Tolerant

Although astrology paints Virgo as a fussy, sometimes humorless, perfectionist, this description isn't accurate. Unlike Gemini, who spits out ideas quickly but with little forethought, a Virgin takes time to think about her options as well as the consequences. If you interrupt her with the latest tale from the grapevine, she'll have to review the process from the beginning. She's not dumb; she's methodical. Her mind processes information in logical order, and she repeats the steps to ensure she hasn't left anything out.

This sounds close to a Libra's mental process, and it is. The difference is that Libra will first try one solution and then another to resolve an issue. Virgo is compelled to try to get it right the first time.

She might be the picture of cool-headed professionalism on the outside, but every Virgo is an introvert at heart who constantly measures herself against everyone else. Thank her when she makes one of her critical observations. Tell her you appreciate her thoughtfulness in helping you to rearrange your workspace more efficiently. Showing her you think she's great just the way she is puts you at the head of this colleague's BOP (Best Office Pal) list.

Keep Your Guard Up

Disruptive Virgos aren't especially ruthless. They're more like the rotten apple that spoils the barrel. If left unchecked, the constant sniping of this bad seed will eventually have the whole workforce snapping at each other like a pack of angry dogs—which, of course, is exactly what he wants to happen. If Virgo's miserable, everyone should be miserable.

She'll complain to you about the rude guy in the next cubicle, then whine to him that she has to pick up your slack. Next, she'll bitch about both of you to the boss, right after she's told someone else what a jerk he is.

If she's unjustly griping about the boss, suggest she file a complaint. If she's bugging you about another colleague, tell her to go to the boss. If you hear that she's dissing you behind your back, confront her. Be professional, but let her know that if she has an issue with you to discuss it with you. Most of us dislike discord, but nothing flattens a passive-aggressive Virgin windbag faster than calling her on her bad behavior.

VIRGO CHEAP SHOTS

- Sabotages projects by omitting important details
- Calls in sick the day of a crucial meeting
- Sulks

Learn to Love Them

Yes, she can be nitpicky, whiny, and irritating. But how many other of your work chums will help you clean out five years' worth of old files or give up her Saturday to help you move your office to the other side of the building?

Your Virgo colleague would rather chat about family or hobbies, or your latest vacation, than listen to the company grapevine. She'll help you find the error in a sales report or track down a caterer for the company Christmas party that's both reputable and bargain priced.

Inside every uptight Virgin is a fun-loving character dying to cut loose. Help her let go by inviting her along on a girls' night out with your friends. She'll appreciate your thoughtfulness, and you'll gain a vibrant new pal.

IF YOU ARE A VIRGO

Talent is cheaper than table salt. What separates the talented individual from the successful one is a lot of hard work.

STEPHEN KING (SEPTEMBER 21)

You're practical, skillful, and self-sufficient. There isn't a job you can't improve on or a boss you can't impress with your painstaking thoroughness and dedication. Your mind is quick to assess a problem and provide a solution. Dedicated and hardworking, you try to avoid power struggles and prefer to focus on doing the best job you can.

So how can you move from middle-of-the-road to the corner office?

Ditch the Minutiae

The old cliché "Don't sweat the small stuff" should be your mantra. You can literally make yourself sick over minutiae that no one else cares about or will even notice. Plus, you create an unreasonable amount of work for yourself. Telling your boss that you're making sure everything's perfect won't help when you put production behind and she has to deal with a screaming customer.

Ask for help and learn to trust your colleagues. Most want to do their best just as you do. It might not be exactly how you would handle it, but if it's on time and correct, then forget it.

Being an Earth sign ruled by Mercury sets up a contradiction in your soul. The Mercury side dreams of freewheeling through life, while the Earth side needs stability. Although you try to set reasonable goals, you can get bogged down with the details and lose opportunities.

Your strength lies in your meticulous attention to research, which results in a expert job. Your weakness is spending way too long in tweaking a task or rechecking your work in fear of making a mistake. Striving for balance is your key to success.

Learn to Listen

You hate being given advice as much as an Aries hates to be last in line at a fire sale. Part of you is offended at the suggestion there might be a better way than yours, and part of you worries that you're going to be revealed as a fraud.

While you take your work seriously and devote yourself to producing consistent quality, this is a dual-edged sword. You can fall behind because you refuse to try new time-saving methods that a colleague might suggest. Instead of welcoming new ideas, you bristle at the thought of someone interfering with your comfortable, albeit cumbersome, routine. This approach will only earn you the reputation as someone who's not interested in moving up.

TIPS FOR SUCCESS

- Don't try to be perfect; no one is
- Learn to accept advice without being offended
- Take more risks

Instead of balking at constructive criticism, welcome it. Use it. Keep what works and forget what doesn't. You'll not only be seen as a true team player who appreciates the help your colleagues offer, you'll help yourself climb the career ladder.

Lighten Up on Yourself

There's an old saying, "The devil is in the details." This devil can drive you nuts. In constantly tweaking your work, trying to ensure you've covered every possible angle, you set an unattainable standard.

As with Cancer, Pisces, and Leo, you try to be all things to all people. Then when you have to choose whether to go home to dinner or burn the midnight oil, your guilt complex kicks in and you give yourself a belly-ache. Keep piling this worry on top of your fear of not measuring up, and you could be headed for the therapist's couch.

Of all the signs, you're by far the most self-critical. The hardest lesson for you to learn is that no one can ever be perfect, not even you. Your challenge is to stop micromanaging yourself. Quit trying to assure that you have all options considered and that contingency plans B, C, D, E, and F are in place before making a move. Nothing's guaranteed. You'll never get off the ground if you insist on having a foolproof plan. Take a leap of faith, Virgo. Even if it doesn't work, you'll see that making mistakes isn't as scary as you think. Once you discover that, you'll discover your wings.

FROM FED UP TO FIRED UP

It's important to give it all you have, while you have the chance.

SHANIA TWAIN (AUGUST 28)

You're honest, scrupulous, and sensitive to those around you. You're adaptable and intelligent, and your systematic approach and eye for detail puts you at the top of your boss's or coworker's most-relied-on-colleague list. Your challenge is to be as discriminating when criticizing others as you are about doing a good job.

Pull in Your Horns

You can be as touchy as a Crab and as territorial as a Leo. The first phrase out of your mouth is usually, "that won't work," and you can balk when someone asks to borrow a pen.

On the other hand, you have no problem telling anyone, including the boss, what you think is wrong with his or her work. Sometimes you not only voice your opinion, you bash people over the head with it. You may think you're trying to help, but you're often viewed as meddling.

Instead of grilling a coworker who wants to borrow your stapler about where he lost his or browbeating a colleague about how you'd handle a situation, stop and think about how you feel when you're on the receiving end of similar behavior.

You're a wonderful problem solver and a giving person. But you'll be taken much more seriously if you stick to helping your colleagues solve the big issues and let them arrange their desktops or filing systems to suit themselves.

Know When to Quit

Of all the Mutable signs, you are the least likely to job-hop. You'll make a plan, brush up your résumé, and give yourself plenty of time to find a good fit before you resign. The trouble is that you can never decide to take the final step and quit. Then when things fall apart, you're forced to scramble to find something that pays the rent.

This can be one significant area of your life where you stifle your inner critic when you should let him have control. A bad boss isn't suddenly going to have an epiphany of kindness. Few companies are going to quit piling on the work as long as you're willing to take it, with or without complaining.

If you feel uncomfortable, analyze your situation with the same critical eye that you apply to your job. Make a list of the advantages (if any) of staying versus leaving. List any options you have to make things better. Weigh your choices, then make a move.

It can be as difficult for you to change course as Libra or any of the Water signs. Unless you do, you could get stuck in Nowhere Land until it's too late.

Ace an Interview

Your perfectly prepared folder of résumé, letters of recommendation, and employment application, plus your neat appearance, will open the door to any top company. The trouble begins when you answer every question with endless details in hopes of covering all the bases.

What's really happening is that you're making the interviewer want to cover her ears. Bombarding a prospective employer with insignificant data is one of the quickest ways to get hustled out the door.

When you're trying to make a point, you have the irritating habit of digressing into an unrelated subject to tell a story that hasn't the slightest link to the present. You might think explaining every detail of how you saved your last four employers beaucoup bucks is impressive. The interviewer is only thinking how she can get through this ordeal without yawning in your face.

Keep it short, to the point, and relevant. Unless the person asks for specifics, don't volunteer them. Your powerful information package and professional appearance gets you more than halfway to landing any job for which you're qualified, Virgo. So remember that, in your case, the less you talk, the better impact you'll make.

Virgo-Friendly Careers

Astrology puts you at the top of the service-industry field. Thanks to your attention to detail, careers such as in a restaurant, hotel, or spa can earn you a five-star rating with clients, as well as lots of money. While you might prefer working either behind the scenes or on your own, what you need is a career that allows you to keep improving your corner of the world.

The following are some other professions that might appeal to your meticulous soul.

Craftsperson

Leather, wood, ceramics, or jewelry making all appeal to your meticulous eye and talent for creating exquisitely detailed one-of-a-kind pieces.

Editor

From the local newspaper to the latest best seller, your dedication to the details helps to produce a superior product. Bonus: Here's where your nit-picking can make you rich.

Veterinarian

You have a natural empathy for helpless animals, which transforms into a near sixth-sense ability to heal them.

Personal Assistant

Whether you're shielding a celebrity from the media or keeping track of the CEO of a Fortune 500 company, your discretion and knack for tracking details makes you an indispensable partner.

Health-Food Guru

Owning a health-food store stocked with medicinal herbs and organically grown food satisfies your need to help people take better care of themselves.

CHAPTER EIGHT

Libra
September 23–October 22

Element:	Air
Quality:	Cardinal
Symbol:	The Scales
Ruler:	Venus
Key word:	Diplomatic
Work-a-tude:	What's the consensus?

INSTANT INSIGHTS

Accent your positive and delete your negative.

DONNA KARAN (OCTOBER 2)

Ruled by Venus, and living in the Seventh House of partnerships, Libra is concerned with beauty, harmony, and all types of human interactions. Sociable Libra thrives in a busy, productive environment and dislikes solitude. Astrology defines Libra's symbol as a set of Scales. Libras are forever trying to seek balance in both their personal and professional lives.

Masculine Cardinal Air Libra is congenial and cooperative. Peacekeeper and diplomat are other terms associated with natives of this sign. The glitch in all this goodness is that beneath the charming exterior, this slyly devious guy is wrangling a way to balance the scales in his favor. Unlike Gemini and Aquarius, who analyze people and situations, Libra rationalizes. His intellect and way with words combine to spit out justifications like a high-powered attorney making excuses for a guilty client. Arguing with a Libra is like trying to convince a Pisces to stand up for himself.

Being a Masculine sign, she'll speak her mind, but in a way that doesn't put her in a compromising position. Her cardinality feels the need to take action, and she'll offer advice or play mediator when she must. However, Libra secretly hates to get involved. Much of the diplomatic attributes that general astrology assigns to a Libra is actually her doing her best to avoid being put in the middle of anything—which, of course, she always somehow manages to do.

Having an emotional character that constantly weighs both sides of an issue and considers every angle gives her the reputation for being fair minded. This is also her Achilles' heel. Her consideration can turn to deliberation, then morph into procrastination, which is how this sign earned the reputation of never being able to make up her mind.

What he is great at is helping others to make up theirs. Your Libra colleague can detach from a situation to see how it really works. He'll give honest feedback and advice on how to compromise. Then he prefers to step out of the picture and let that person make the final decision.

FAMOUS PEACE-LOVING LIBRAS

- Alfred Nobel, founder of the Nobel Prize (October 21)
- Rev. Jesse Jackson, human rights activist (October 8)
- Hugh Jackman, actor (October 12)

Cardinal Aries can lead by intimidation. Cardinal Cancer needs control. Cardinal Capricorn takes calculated action. Cardinal Libra, however, wants to be the guiding force behind a team effort. Her Seventh House soul needs to work and live closely with other people to feel complete.

LIBRA ON THE JOB

I wouldn't dream of working on something that didn't make my gut rumble.

KATE WINSLET (OCTOBER 5)

A soft-spoken Libra coworker will make you feel at home if you're new and give you steady support as a long-term office mate. She's smart, disciplined, and totally in tune with what's going on around her.

She's outgoing and easy to get to know. This is another sign that will be your buddy at work and, off the clock, your shop-til-you-drop pal. She organizes birthday parties and orders the flowers for special occasions. Win her over by remembering her birthday or bringing her an inexpensive gift for no reason, such as a notepad with her name on it. Considerate Libra appreciates thoughtfulness in others.

As does Cancer, Ms. Libra decorates her workspace with personal items, but her Venus-ruled soul strives for beauty and balance, so you're unlikely to see a clutter of mementos or photos push-pinned to a cork-board. She's chic like Capricorn.

This colleague might act more sociable than serious. However, he has a keen intellect, knows what he wants, and has a plan in place to achieve it. Due to his vacillating nature, it might take him longer to get there. But Libra is a Cardinal (action) sign, so even if he appears to be stuck in neutral, he's always making headway.

Managing a Libra
Communication Is Key

Stick a Libra in a corner with no people contact, and she'll wilt like last week's flowers. Unlike Scorpio, Pisces, or Aquarius, who can prefer to work alone, Libra thrives in a mainstream situation. Let her help develop a marketing plan or put her on a design team. With her Venus eye for style, she'll rack up clothing sales, and repeat customers, by expertly helping them find their perfect look.

Libra is the zodiac's schmoozer. Whether he works in a department store, pet store, or is your sympathetic bartender, Libra performs best when working with the public. Let him wine and dine clients or negotiate contracts. Keep your line of communication direct and open with your Libra employee. His opinion is worth hearing, and he has one on every issue. He'll appreciate your guidance on how to handle a situation and rely on you to make decisions after he's given you several options.

Libra is as loyal as Taurus, smart as Gemini, and friendly as Leo. Treat her fairly, nudge her into taking more responsibility, and reward her with a personal perk now and then, and you'll have a star performer on your team.

Keep Them Enthused

Every sign has its share of power players, including Libra. However, the average Libran prefers to be the power behind the scenes. Don't misinterpret—Libra's willing to take on any responsibility you delegate and will do a stellar job. What they can prefer not to do is be the person who makes the final decisions.

Your Libra would rather be the advice giver, debater, and to play devil's advocate. She's excellent at taking either viewpoint on an issue and outlining the pros and cons. Let her be your sounding board, and she'll feel valued.

Even-tempered Libra excels at handling grievances, sorting out multilayered problems, or stepping in anywhere an impartial attitude is required. Put her in charge of a performance improvement or quality customer service team. She'll evaluate a process, listen fairly to concerns, and then put together a cohesive, unbiased report. Your bonus is that she'll also suggest multiple solutions, any one of which will benefit the most people possible.

Whether he's your floor manager or the parts man behind the counter, let your Libra brainstorm strategy with the bigwigs. His objective perspective can add valuable insight.

Don't Get Snake-Charmed

There's an old saying: "Give an inch, and they'll take a mile." Memorize it. Libra's soothing personality is rather like a Venus flytrap. She instinctively knows how to lull even her most intimidating adversary into a false sense of security. This sign was born knowing how to charm her way through life. She'll start with praise to put you off guard, ask the favor, and then close with that beaming smile and another head pat. She can also instigate a feud with a coworker and make it sound like she's the victim, not the perpetrator.

If you aren't alert, the extra half-hour at lunch turns into an afternoon off with pay. The half-day Friday off stretches into a four-day weekend. Libra can be chronically late to work with a hundred different excuses that all sound sincere.

Despite having an air of vulnerability, Libra is a Cardinal sign, and Cardinal signs always push for control. You must stick to the rules. Remind him that he has to follow them. You can sincerely (or not) show regret that you have to dock his check for missing all those hours. Throw in that you have to be fair to all the staff and watch him wince. Despite his astrological rep for being the world's most cooperative guy, Libra secretly only likes to compromise when it's in his favor. But don't forget to pat his head before you send him back to work.

Surviving Boss Libra

Know What You're Dealing With

Whether he's a blue-collar line supervisor or a white-collar executive, the Libra boss is an excellent motivator. Even handed and disciplined, this boss is dedicated to running an efficient and harmonious workplace. Other than his frustrating knack for taking a brain-draining amount of time to make decisions, Boss Libra is one of the best.

Well, except for another irritating habit. He rarely takes sides, even on your behalf. He'll expect you to exhaust every effort before he gets personally involved. If the situation is truly bad, he'll mull it over. Although he's a wonderful mediator, he's not out to prove who's right or wrong, as a Scorpio or an Aries boss can be. So even if you have a solid case, he'll probably ask you to compromise in some way to keep the peace.

She'll call attention to your errors calmly and won't be overly critical at your annual review. Great, huh? Not quite. You might never know exactly where you stand with Boss Libra, which can rattle your confidence in your job security. Libra likes it that way. She figures it keeps you on your toes.

So how can you impress this smooth, evasive character?

Be Sincere

Boss Libra is a champ at spotting phony behavior. That's because she's so good at playing both sides of the fence. She's skilled at office politics, and she's prepared to mentally and verbally spar with anyone she must in order to protect her business or her staff. The perception is that she likes the game playing. Truth is, she doesn't. What she appreciates is candid debate. Head games not only annoy her, they insult her intelligence.

This is one boss who will seek your input and appreciate your honest feedback. If he hands you a project, shape it the way you think it works best. When he runs one of his ideas by you, give him your straightforward analysis. Never try to second-guess him. He gets that from everyone else.

Boss Libra appreciates intellectual stimulation, not mindless rhetoric. Be his sounding board. Caution him when you think he's headed in the wrong direction, and don't be afraid to make suggestions. Whether he uses them or not, he'll see you as a priceless asset that he can depend on for the truth.

LIBRA WORDS TO LIVE BY

"Don't give up. Don't lose hope. Don't sell out."
—Christopher Reeve (September 25)

"Luck is a dividend of sweat. The more you sweat, the luckier you get."
—Ray Kroc, founder of McDonald's Corporation (October 5)

Expect Delays

A Leo boss wants his way no matter what. A Gemini boss will start, then drop, a dozen ideas. Boss Libra, however, will analyze every angle, canvas the company gathering opinions, weigh each one, and then swing from one opposite view to the other. After all those time-eating gyrations, he might decide to let the whole thing simmer on the back burner for a few more weeks.

When a Libra has a difficult decision or can't make up her mind, she has a way of dropping the subject altogether until something forces her hand. She might let it slide until her boss barks. Or she might wait until the last second so that she's forced to use the less-efficient, but quicker, fix, rather than the elaborate plan she labored over.

Your job is to go with the flow, to a point. Stay organized so that you can hand her a copy of Plan A, B, or C on a moment's notice. Keep her on track with deadline reminders and a nudge if she's ignoring the issue. She might grumble, but she'll appreciate your dedication, and you might even get her off the stick.

Coping with a Libra Coworker

There's one sure way to get along with any Libra in the universe: Let them know that you are willing to meet them halfway. Balance is one of Libra's key words. This colleague doesn't like to make waves and gets anxious if anyone else rocks the boat. Your Libra coworker is always willing to negotiate. If you are, too, you'll forge a solid bond.

Be Willing to Give a Little

Your Libra colleague can be irritatingly argumentative. He'll nitpick an issue to death, put it back together, and then pull it apart again. That's because his internal system of checks and balances compels him to find the way that gives the most benefit to as many people as possible—most of the time.

As long as it doesn't affect your input, let her choose how to set up a presentation or arrange product on a display counter. The smallest concession—such as letting her take her break first or agreeing to alternate lunch hours—might not make a difference to you, but it lets your Libra office chum know that you're considerate of her feelings.

Compromise on the most mundane level will earn you his friendship, and when the bigger issues come up, Libra won't forget to swing his scales back in your favor.

Keep Your Guard Up

A bad Libra can make the most shallow compliment sound as if she's your biggest fan. If she wants the plum assignment you're about to get handed, she'll appear to be *so* happy for you. She might say something like, "That's wonderful news. You've always been a hard worker, even if you could learn more about bringing projects in under budget." This sign has perfected the art of dishing out left-handed compliments.

After she's flashed you that sweet smile and offered her help anytime you should need it, she'll march directly to the boss and tell him exactly the same thing, all in the guise of being a team player. But the only team she's interested in is her party of one.

The best way to stop this double dealer is to gush your thanks for her support right back at her. Then never accept any kind of "help."

LIBRA CHEAP SHOTS

- Gives phony praise
- Pushes for more
- Tells the boss you're incompetent

Learn to Love Them

Who can resist a Libra? She'll turn on her high-beam charm and take you under her wing to show you the ropes. She knows the best place to go for a gourmet lunch, and where to find a posh club that serves unadvertised half-price drinks at happy hour. This thoughtful colleague will remember the kind of candy you like and bring you a box as a thank you for covering for her. She'll return the favor and pick up the slack when you're under pressure.

Whether she's selling jewelry or helping senior citizens plan a healthy diet, this colleague bounces into work every morning ready to go and eager to please. She's fun, witty, smart, and cool in a crisis.

Your Libra coworker will keep you updated on the latest changes in company policy and help you outwit a rival. One of her quirks is to ask a small favor now and then to test your loyalty. Pitch in without hesitation, because once a Libra becomes your friend, she'll stick by you forever.

IF YOU ARE A LIBRA

I wake up every morning believing that today is going to be better than yesterday.

WILL SMITH (SEPTEMBER 25)

You're logical, detached, and, despite your Venus-influenced character, rarely let your heart rule over your head. There isn't a boss or colleague you can't charm or a problem you can't solve. You're always on the lookout for ways to make things run better, cheaper, or smoother. When you get an assignment, you don't consider it finished until you've satisfied yourself that you've done the best job possible.

So what do you need to do to see that you give yourself the best career possible?

Know When to Get Involved

You can't stand to see another colleague perform what you judge as sloppy work. You offer to help, but your friendly critiques can come across as nit-picking, similar to a Virgo efficiency expert. I know a Libra who was so exasperated by a clerk's careless filing system that she went in on a Saturday and rearranged the entire cabinet in perfect alphabetical order. It would have been a nice gesture had she checked with the clerk before assuming he needed, or wanted, her help. Instead of getting her colleague's gratitude, he complained to the boss. He was right.

Because someone handles things differently than you doesn't mean that it's wrong. Save your comments for big issues or when you catch a serious error.

Sometimes, no matter how hard you try to stay out of either a personal or a professional dispute, you end up in the middle with both sides angry at you. That's because instead of coming across as truly impartial, you give the wrong impression that you agree with each of the arguing parties. When that gets around, and it always does, each side thinks you're spying for the other. Although you like being a counselor and hearing the juicy tiff firsthand, try to avoid commenting other than to suggest they sit down together and talk. Or take it to the supervisor. Then you'll be recognized for the smart cookie you are and not just another meddling coworker.

TIPS FOR SUCCESS

- Dare to be impulsive
- Respect other people's time
- Stifle your jealously

Curb Your Envy

As a Masculine Cardinal sign, you're naturally competitive, although with much more subtlety than either Aries or Capricorn, and with less manipulation than Cancer. Being ruled by Venus gives you a subconscious sense that you're higher on the privilege scale than most people. Add this up, and you can get downright peevish when someone does better than you, even if it's your closest pal at work.

Everyone's jealous now and then, but it's one of your worst traits. When you envy a colleague's success, you can spit out a kudo that sounds more like a verbal right cross. You might think that no one will notice because you sound gracious. You don't. Everyone within earshot will know exactly how you feel, and your false praise will come across as phony and juvenile. There's no quicker way to lose popularity points.

Do yourself a favor if you can't feel genuine pleasure for a colleague's achievements: Take the age-old advice and don't say anything at all.

Put Away Your "I'm Available" Sign

You're another one of the natural flirts of the zodiac. Whether you're twinkling at the boss's cute assistant or making a play for a hot newly hired hunk, you want to be first to put your brand on a potential playmate.

In today's world, it's perfectly acceptable to date a coworker, which you will usually do with discretion. Hooking up on company time isn't your biggest detriment to success; incessant flirting is how you shoot yourself in the foot. There's a fine line between being seen as charming and being viewed as a phony kiss-up.

A Libra I once knew was smart, good looking, and outstanding at her job. She also couldn't resist turning on her high-beam charm at every opportunity. From cooing at the UPS guy to gushing over a coworker's new-baby pictures, she tried hard to earn the rep as Ms. Congeniality, but behind her back she was known as Ms. Diabetes. Her fawning backfired big time the day she attempted to straighten the boss's tie before a meeting and he snapped her head off in front of everyone.

Although your Venus-ruled nature needs to be popular and gain group adoration, to be taken seriously in your career, you must learn to walk that fine line between being captivating and cloying.

FROM FED UP TO FIRED UP

If I had to sum up in one word what makes a good manager, I'd say decisiveness . . . in the end you have to set a timetable and act.

Lee Iacocca (October 15)

You can turn the surliest coworker into a friend and make your boss think he or she can't function without your skillful guidance. You make an extra effort to strive for fairness for your colleagues as well as yourself, and your quiet diplomacy can soothe the angriest customer. Your challenge is not to get bogged down trying to cover every angle. While you're debating with yourself, the rest of the world is passing by.

Don't Dawdle

You know you're not indecisive. I know you're not indecisive. Any serious astrology book will confirm that you're not indecisive. But you have the reputation for it because of the length of time it can take you to finish a task. In your personal life, this trait works when you want to cook a gourmet dinner to impress your latest lover or are searching for the perfect cocktail dress. At work, it can be disastrous.

"Time is of the essence" is a common cliché that you should memorize. At work you'll rarely have the luxury of unlimited time to rearrange shelf stock or investigate a project from six different perspectives. There are other coworkers who might be waiting for your input, or budget figures, or sales stock. Along with Virgo and Taurus, you hate to rush. However, endless nit-picking over which purse goes where on the sales rack makes you look obsessive, not efficient.

Whether you mean it or not, when you make others wait while you fiddle around, you not only hold up progress, you show a lack of respect for their time. You're a savvy soul. Be aware of how your actions affect your coworkers and don't get so carried away with the small details that you forget the big picture.

Know When to Quit

You hate to give up on anything, so you tend to stay put in a dead-end job longer than you should. You aren't someone who makes decisions lightly, which is admirable. However, wasting your gifts of communication and cooperation on an employer who doesn't appreciate you is the worst self-sabotage.

If your boss is a bitch, you'll try to rationalize her behavior, work harder to please her, and hope for the best. If you're overworked and underpaid you'll voice your concern, but you'll usually stick with the company out of loyalty, thinking your diligence will eventually get rewarded. What happens is that you get blindsided by getting fired because you hung in too long. Another way you sabotage yourself is with your near-eternal dithering about whether you should make a move. Maybe things will get better where you are. Maybe the new job will be worse. While you're weighing your options, the opportunities are being snapped up by other people.

Networking is a painless way to find prospects, so use your extensive social and professional contacts to put the word out that you're looking. Your friends will be eager to help, and you can feel free to follow up on anything that looks good—or not.

Ace an Interview

Your air of cool confidence and ability to make anyone feel special, combined with your impeccable credentials, gets you on any interviewer's A-list of candidates. Your knack for knowing what to say and when to say it further heightens your chances of landing the job you seek.

You flub it by failing to recognize the fine line between relaxed, friendly interaction and coming across as too effusive or, worse, flirty. Don't try to shift the focus by asking the interviewer personal questions or going off on a tangent about your own life. You might think you're forming a bond, but the interviewer thinks that your up-close-and-personal act is just that—an act. Along with Pisces, you're one of the touchy-feely signs. You hug friends, pat coworkers on the arm, and will even pick lint off a bigwig's suit. This is fine around people who know you, but never squeeze the guy's arm who's grilling you about why you want to work for him. He might think you want more than a job.

Sometimes an interviewer will ask you how you would handle a situation. Stifle the urge to give her three or four scenarios and instead choose the one you think is the best. Otherwise, your twenty-minute dissertation on the pros and cons will sound pretentious. Plus, do your either–or–maybe–it depends routine, and you'll come across as unsure of yourself.

All in all, you make a wonderful first impression because your people skills are natural and you are genuinely at ease around anyone. Talk less and be as succinct as possible, and you'll ace any interview.

Libra-Friendly Careers

Ruled by Venus, you bring the same creative touch to your job as does Taurus. Further, your skill at reading other people's motives and talent for debate is a successful combination no matter what you decide to do. What you need is intellectual stimulation, communication, and to be independent within an interdependent group.

The following are a few possibilities you might like.

Interior Decorator

You love beautiful things—and spending other people's money. What better way to combine both than turning your clients' homes or offices into showplaces?

Agent

Your excellent people skills, cleverness at negotiations, and genuine interest in your clients' careers are a winning combination for megasuccess.

Movie Star

Eternal romantic that you are, what better way to be able to act out your greatest fantasies and receive the adoration of millions of fans?

Matchmaker

Playing Cupid appeals to your love of happy endings, and your analytical approach to determining the right fit in matching couples could make you rich and famous.

Civil Rights Activist

Your belief in equality and harmony, and your gift for arguing passionately on behalf of others, makes you a natural at fighting for justice.

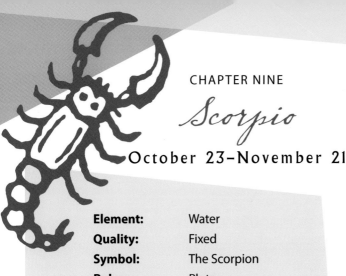

CHAPTER NINE

Scorpio

October 23–November 21

Element:	Water
Quality:	Fixed
Symbol:	The Scorpion
Ruler:	Pluto
Key word:	Tenacious
Work-a-tude:	Failure is not an option.

INSTANT INSIGHTS

Normal is not something to aspire to, it's something to get away from.

JODIE FOSTER (NOVEMBER 19)

Scorpios have the scariest reputation in the zodiac. Most of it's a bad rap. Yes, they are tough. Yes, they can be vengeful. Yes, they can be brutally frank. But never forget that this is a Water sign, and all water babies are sensitive.

Think of it this way: A real scorpion is frightening to see; however, it's not an attack creature. It only stings when threatened, and as a last resort after trying every other way to escape its predator. The human version is exactly the same. She'll usually stay out of office feuds unless someone takes aim at her first. Then, duck. An infuriated Scorpio can unleash a tirade that will make the meanest Aries drop and roll.

FAMOUS POWERFUL SCORPIOS

- Hillary Rodham Clinton, U.S. Secretary of State (October 26)
- Bill Gates, founder of Microsoft (October 28)
- Martin Scorsese, Oscar-winning director (November 17)

The other part of a Scorpion's scary status comes from its home base on the zodiac wheel, the Eighth House of death, sex, and other people's money. Pluto, the planet of destruction and resurrection, rules Scorpio. In mythology, Pluto is the lord of the underworld who guarded the gates of Hades. Very powerful stuff.

Your Scorpio coworker is just as powerful. He's self-motivated and self-assured. Although *secretive* is the common descriptor of his personality, *private* is a better choice. A Scorpion is private about his personal life and totally discreet on the job.

Fixed Air Aquarius has cast-iron beliefs. Things can be either black or white. Fixed Earth Taurus's security lays in gathering possessions. Fixed Fire Leo's nature is to take responsibility for others whether they want help or not. Fixed Water Scorpio, however, has fixed emotions and is easily wounded. Be kind to him, and he'll be generous and kind to you. Treat him badly, and he'll cut you off without a second glance.

SCORPIO ON THE JOB

The person with the best job in the country is the vice president. All he has to do is get up every morning and say, "How is the president?"
— WILL ROGERS (NOVEMBER 4)

A Scorpio will treat her coworkers with the same respect she gives her friends. She's discreet, trustworthy, and loyal. This is one sign that will ride out the rough times by taking a pay cut to help prevent a coworker from losing his job.

Contrary to the doom and gloom descriptions that astrology has tagged these natives with, Scorpios are fun loving and have a wicked sense of humor. One of the funniest colleagues I ever had was a Scorpio guy who could do a dead-on imitation of anyone, including the boss.

If you want an honest answer, ask your Scorpio coworker. She doesn't play both sides of the fence like Gemini, and she won't blurt out the first thing that comes to mind as a Sagittarius can. She will appraise the situation and tell you the truth as she sees it. It might not be what you want to hear, but it won't be a verbal ass pat or useless chatter. How refreshing is that?

Managing a Scorpion
Don't Take Advantage

You might never discover what's going on in a Scorpio's head, and if you're smart, you won't pry. He'll value your appreciation, but you won't win him over with extra perks or compliments. If you dangle a reward, be sure to pay up when he's met your expectations.

When he's after something, he's as tenacious as a Leo with his eye on the executive suite and as subtle as a Libra sucking you into a trap. The difference is that Scorpio rarely makes waves. He'll take a surprising amount of criticism or tolerate outrageous hours—as long as you can help him reach his goal. This isn't advice to try to work your Scorpion to death—it's a warning. Treating him badly will backfire once he gets what he wants. Never burn bridges with this sign. Although his symbol is a scorpion, this native's memory is more like an elephant. Whether it's your support or your neglect, a Scorpio doesn't forget. Commit this fact to *your* memory, and you'll save yourself a whole lot of trouble.

Keep Them Enthused

Your Scorpio staff member doesn't fall apart under pressure. She won't expect you to be her therapist, mother, or confidant. As with Taurus and Cancer, her job is a means to an end. Whether that's paying the rent and supporting a family or breaking through the glass ceiling, she's on her own mission, not yours.

Give her challenges that require concentration or investigative research. Make her a client advocate for confidential issues such as helping patients untangle an insurance billing mess. Put her on the audit trail to nail a cheat. She works well with the public, but let your Libra, Aries, or Leo handle the two-hour lunches or front office. Your Scorpio likes to get involved at a deeper level.

He's capable of running a department or division with minimum supervision, and you can count on him to keep the ball rolling when you're gone. He'll respect your position, even if he doesn't always agree with your opinion.

With a little forethought and a reserved approach, you'll earn your Scorpio's trust and loyalty. Once you do, you'll forge an unbreakable, and unbeatable, bond.

Beware a Battle of Wills

While every Fixed sign thinks that his way is the best way, the Scorpion is the most strong willed. Arguing won't help. Even if you're as rational as the most diplomatic Libra, any Scorpio worth her salt can make you feel like the unlucky target of a prosecuting attorney.

Unlike Leo, he won't toss his keys on your desk and storm out if he doesn't get his way. This is one sign that isn't about to put himself out of a job by acting rash. However, you can save each of you a ton of angst, and keep your Scorpio's respect, if you don't bark orders. If you're making a change, firmly but quietly state the new procedure, responsibility, or rule. Then listen to his opinion. A Scorpio's brain might not spit out ideas at the speed of sound like Gemini or Sagittarius, but more often than not, his proposals pay off. Whether you use his suggestions or not, he'll respect that you're the boss and that you at least considered his point of view. A little temperance goes a long way with this stubborn, sensitive sign.

Surviving Boss Scorpion
Know What You're Dealing With

A Taurus boss is money conscious. A Cancer boss can be a dictator. A Leo boss hates lies. Boss Scorpion, however, is a blend of all three, plus she has her own special quality of being slightly paranoid. On the surface, this boss is friendly, chatty, and seems flexible. In truth, she's complex, hard to read, and always knows what's going on—always. Nothing escapes Boss Scorpion's notice.

He's driven to do the best job he can and is suspicious of anyone who doesn't work as hard. Where a Sagittarius boss might ignore a little Internet shopping on a slow afternoon, Boss Scorpio might decide to give you the afternoon off without pay.

Money is important. But whether he's the lone manager of a small-town business or the chief investigative journalist for a top news magazine, a Scorpion's real motivator is power. It doesn't matter if he's directing the action up front or pulling the strings from behind the scenes. He doesn't need prestige, like Capricorn craves. Boss Scorpio wants total control and won't let anything stand in his way to achieve it.

Help him achieve it by keeping your head down, getting your work done, and playing by his rules. Once you earn his trust, you earn his protection. When you're protected by a Scorpion, nothing much can stand in your way, either.

SCORPIO WORDS TO LIVE BY

"You can never quit."
—Ted Turner (November 19)

"Attack life. It's going to kill you anyway."
—Unknown

Keep It Confidential

A couple of things to remember when working for a Scorpio: never spill a confidence, and never confide too much personal stuff. Breaking the first rule will break this boss's trust. Once that's gone, it's time to look for another job. Fast. Breaking the second could put you at the mercy of a manipulating Scorpion. That's rare, but it's worth knowing. This doesn't mean that you can't be yourself. You must. She accepts people for who they are. Besides, she'll see through a phony facade quicker than a Capricorn can spot a designer suit knockoff.

Another thing that drives Boss Scorpion crazy is when you act like you know something he doesn't. It's part of his paranoia. He has secrets, and no one else is allowed to. So if you're whispering on the phone or suddenly click off e-mail when he walks in, he'll suspect whatever you're doing is aimed at him. Even the most rational Scorpio can have the nagging feeling that someone's out to get him. Keep this boss happy by always being open and direct. Give him facts, not speculation. Back up the facts with numbers. Be confidential, even with the small stuff.

It's not easy working for a Scorpion, but once she sees that you're dedicated and serious about doing a good job, you'll discover the other side of this enigmatic character—the one that's sympathetic and kind.

Be Resourceful

Scorpios have as curious a nature as Gemini. The difference is that Twins skim the surface, while Scorpio is the detective of the zodiac. His Twelfth

House soul loves to probe into mysteries, unravel puzzles, and ferret out information that no one else has. The more this boss can learn about a rival, a rumor, or a potential money-making plan, the better.

Keep your ears and eyes open for opportunities that can help her achieve a goal. She's not interested in gossip. Unless you have facts, don't bother her. Dig deep when researching a project. If you uncover new knowledge or a different twist on a common idea, you'll gain her respect.

Coping with a Scorpio Coworker

A Scorpio coworker is an enigma. Pleasant, team-spirited, and friendly on the surface, this workmate is reserved, cautious, and emotionally guarded inside. The best way to win a Scorpion over is with time and discretion. Treat this colleague with respect, keep the conversation casual, and be someone on whom she can count. Once she does let her guard down, you'll find a friend.

Approach with Caution

A good way to make friends with a Scorpio is to be friendly, but keep your distance. Invite her to coffee only after you've worked together for a few weeks. Scorpios mistrust someone who rushes toward any type of emotional involvement, friendship included.

All Water signs are thin-skinned. Scorpio is hypersensitive but covers it so well that even he will deny there's a problem until he explodes. Casual joking, as you'd do with a Sagittarius, doesn't always work with a Scorpion.

I once watched as a Scorpio became increasingly fed up with a loud coworker who embarrassed the Scorpion in front of her peers. The other woman tried to laugh it off, but in less than a heartbeat and without raising her voice, the Scorpio launched into a vitriolic flare-up that left everyone openmouthed. Until that moment, none of us had witnessed Scorpio anger. She'd been backed into a corner that she'd tried to avoid for months and was finally pushed beyond her limit. It's a good reminder that this sign can be every bit as volatile as a Leo running amok. But if you make the effort, you'll make an office pal you can count on anytime, any place.

Keep Your Guard Up

American humorist Will Rogers, a Scorpio, said, "We don't know what we want, but we're willing to bite somebody to get it." It's a wise piece of advice to follow when working with a Scorpion.

If she's after your job, she'll use subtle subterfuge, like Cancer and Libra. Not because she's adverse to direct conflict, but because she'll try to cover her own butt at the same time she's frying yours. The only time she'll attack is if she catches you alone. Should you complain to the boss, she has zero conscience about lying through her teeth that anything happened.

A rotten Scorpion is the kind of enemy you hope you don't run into in the elevator. He'll know exactly which of your buttons to push to try to draw you into a verbal battle, and he won't hesitate to start jabbing the moment he sees you. Don't give him the satisfaction. Ignoring a Scorpion on a rampage is the quickest way to defuse a potential battle. When he can't sting you with his words, you take away his power.

SCORPIO CHEAP SHOTS

- Attacks you privately while maintaining a professional public facade
- Uses your secrets against you
- Discredits you behind your back

As for her behind-your-back plotting, unless you're screwing up and she has the proof, or she's the boss's relative, ignore that, too. Even bad Scorpions aren't stupid. She won't attack if she can't provoke you. She'll learn she can't get to you and withdraw.

Learn to Love Them

There's no better colleague to have on your side than an astute and sneaky Scorpio. She'll help you expose a workplace spy or track down an old boyfriend. When you're overworked, she'll share the load. When you're ready to rock 'n' roll, she'll be your designated driver.

She'll watch your back and stay out of your space when you're busy. This sign won't bore you with superficial babble or try to monopolize your time with trivial problems. The Scorpion is intense, determined, and has a wholehearted approach to both work and life. She's slow to commit as a friend or an on-the-job confidante, but once she does you'll never have to worry about getting stabbed in the back. Scorpio believes in loyalty. In this day of cutthroat competition and two-faced coworkers, that's as good as gold.

IF YOU ARE A SCORPIO

Success is a lousy teacher. It seduces smart people into thinking they can't lose.
BILL GATES (OCTOBER 28)

You tackle everything you do with the single-minded purpose of succeeding. As the saying goes, "Failure's not an option." You're strong willed and self-sufficient. You don't hesitate to go after what you want, and there isn't a coworker you can't turn into an ally or a boss you can't convince that he'd be lost without you.

So how can you escape a rut-bound nine to five and find a stellar career?

Forget about It

Your Fixed Water emotional structure is similar to a deep, still well. It holds whatever you dump in. Unlike a Fire sign, who blows up and then forgets the issue, or an Air sign, who argues its points and then moves on, you tend to emotionally hang on to every letdown, loss, or aggravation.

So the boss was a bitch yesterday. So what? Or the Leo in the next cubicle made a snarky remark about your miniskirt. Let it go. Some Scorpios hold on to every real or imagined insult until that's all they think or talk about. If you have this trait, remember that dwelling on each office tiff, or argument you don't win, sucks time that you could be using to focus on getting ahead. When that happens, the people you're pissed at win by default.

Rein in Your Suspicions

No one questions that you're both intuitive and sensitive. You also can be paranoid that people are only nice to you because they want something from you. Could that be because sometimes your motives can be a little devious?

Lift the emotional load in your head by letting down your barrier at least far enough to form some casual friendships at work. Most people are so busy with their own career path that they have neither the time nor the inclination to stab you in the back. Most wouldn't, anyway.

You tend to stick to yourself or form one or two close work relationships. When you do that, you keep yourself out of the insider loop that could lead to getting the scoop on an upcoming promotion. Even casual networking across departments is a plus. You'll make new contacts and maybe a new friend. Reach out to your colleagues, and you can't lose. When it comes to the information exchange, you invariably get the most for the least.

Instead of scrutinizing every gesture of help or friendship, try taking them at face value. You don't have to become anyone's instant best pal. But when you doubt every kindness, or cut yourself off from every available source of information, you're the only one who loses.

TIPS FOR SUCCESS

- Take control of you, instead of trying to control those around you
- Control your suspicious nature
- Be aware of your negative side

Control Your Negative Outlook

We've all had upheavals at work and in life. We've all run into bad bosses and backstabbing coworkers. We've all been betrayed. The problem is that you often act as if you're waiting for the other shoe to drop. Being prepared with a contingency plan is one thing, but having the "*if something can go wrong, it will*" outlook is total self-sabotage. As with Capricorn, your negativity can stifle your career. While you're hesitating because of a real or imagined obstacle, someone else is making his move.

You have a deep optimism. Otherwise you couldn't survive all the drama that most of you Scorpios have lived through. When you learn to deliberately let it out, you'll discover that you're a force of nature that can't be stopped.

FROM FED UP TO FIRED UP

It's important not to limit yourself. You can do whatever you love to do.

RYAN GOSLING (NOVEMBER 12)

Focused, determined, and strong, few situations intimidate you. You're at your best when the challenge is the toughest, and there isn't a crisis, or a boss, that you can't handle. Your coworkers know that they can rely on your help, and your boss knows she can trust you with the most confidential information. Your challenge is to give both yourself and others the benefit of the doubt.

Lighten Up on Yourself

You're known as one of the toughest adversaries in the universe, but the person you often beat up on the most is yourself. Unlike a Fire sign that rushes headlong into any situation, you're good at picking both your goals and your battles. Where you get sidetracked is when you take on so much responsibility that you constantly walk the fine line between a breakthrough and a burnout.

You'll do whatever it takes to get the job done and can handle a workload that would stagger a Capricorn. You get in trouble when you assume that you're the one who needs to pick up the slack. You also wrongly believe that if you don't, your boss or coworkers will think you're lazy. Not true. Don't hesitate to ask for help when you need it. Daring to push the limit is admirable, but pushing yourself to the brink can damage your career, not to mention your health. When you try to do it all, you get so lost in busywork that you can lose sight of your dreams.

Know When to Quit

Your Scorpio nature is like a deep well. Once dug in, either in a relationship or at a job, it takes a near Herculean effort to move you. As a Fixed sign, you dislike change. As a Water sign, breaking any emotional attachment, even a bad one, causes you high anxiety. This double whammy can keep you in a dead-end job too long.

You're the most resilient sign in the zodiac. As a Scorpio, you've faced plenty of serious crises in life and managed to survive, even thrive. You have Pluto's strength of rejuvenation that gives you the will to start over if you must and end up in a better spot. However, you shoot yourself in the foot by being so reluctant to initiate change that you are likely to pass up an opportunity, even when it's handed to you.

In astrological theory, you have the reputation for great timing, waiting and watching until the right moment before you make a move. In reality, you hate to give up. Your loyalty to a boss or a company can become a barrier when you know that you should quit, but you feel guilty about leaving. If this sounds like you, remember the boss has his own agenda, and losing you to a competitor or a promotion isn't on it. Being loyal to yourself first is the way to take real control of your career.

Ace an Interview

Few things intimidate you, and applying for a job isn't one of them. Your direct eye contact and firm handshake signal that you are serious and professional. Your disarming smile and attentive attitude impress any potential employer. What you dislike is answering questions.

Like Taurus, you can turn what's supposed to be a relaxed dialogue into a grueling cross-examination. The difference is that Taurus is reacting from nervous tension, and you think that any question is an invasion of your privacy. You might have the less-is-more approach to disclosing personal information, but in an interview, one-word answers make the person you're talking with think you're either unsociable or uninterested. Either assumption is a sure way to get the boot in record time.

Help yourself by being prepared with a few general answers to questions you know you're going to hear. "Why are you leaving your current job?" "What attracted you to our company?" "Tell me about your qualifications." Don't worry about talking too much; that's not one of your faults.

You have drive, ambition, and are rarely without a plan. If you loosen up a bit, you'll ace every interview and every job you land on your way to the top.

Scorpio-Friendly Careers

Astrology lists you in the heavy-hitting-jobs column: careers that call for precision and concentration, such as a surgeon or an engineer, or ones where you can exercise your powers of observation, like forensic pathology. This doesn't mean that a Scorpio can't be a florist, entertainer, or chef. What works best for you is a job that makes the most of your ability to dig out the facts, then put them together in a plan that benefits everyone around you.

The following are some possibilities.

Confidential Assistant

No one is better at keeping secrets than you. That's why you're an indispensable sidekick in any job that calls for discretion, confidentiality, and absolute trust.

Crime Scene Investigator (CSI)

Your sixth sense, love of solving mysteries, and talent for uncovering hidden clues that others might miss makes you the CSI whom everyone wants on their team.

Real Estate Agent / Developer

You're great at seeing the potential in a fixer-upper or a bare piece of land with a view. Because your private space is important to you, and you understand true value, you take extra care to ensure that your clients find the perfect home at the right price.

Chief of Security

Protecting those who can't protect themselves is an integral part of your character. Whether you own your own security systems company or are head of a team safeguarding the country, your clients can feel safe knowing that nothing can escape your scrutiny.

Mystery or Horror Writer

Tapping into the dark side of your character to create intricately woven plots or devilishly scream-worthy stories can send you straight to the top of the best-seller list.

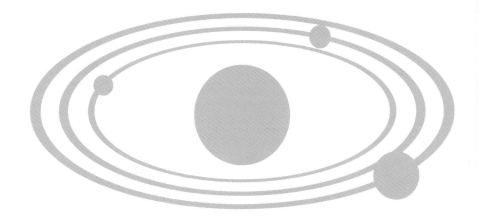

CHAPTER TEN

Sagittarius

November 22–December 21

Element:	Fire
Quality:	Mutable
Symbol:	The Archer
Ruler:	Jupiter
Key word:	Versatile
Work-a-tude:	Let me handle this . . . and this . . . and this . . .

INSTANT INSIGHTS

Here's to the confusion of our enemies!

FRANK SINATRA (DECEMBER 12)

Mutable Masculine Fire Sagittarius is the most optimistic sign in the zodiac. Your average Archer has a wonderful sense of humor and can be the biggest clown at the annual picnic or the first to laugh at her own mistakes.

Sagittarius lives in the Ninth House on the zodiac wheel. This is the hangout of philosophers, adventurers, and higher learning. While his Gemini colleague is concerned with immediate tasks and initiating new ideas, a Jupiter-ruled Archer looks at the big picture and how what happens today can affect future business. *Big* is a word astrology associates with Sagittarius: Bighearted. Big dreams. Big deals.

What you see is what you get with an Archer. Outspoken as Aquarius and more footloose than an Aries, your Sagittarius work chum is quick to make friends and quicker to speak her mind. It's the latter that gets her in trouble. A Scorpion might be brutally honest, but your Archer can be thoughtlessly so. Instead of retreating as a Water sign might or deliberating as an Earth sign could, she blasts full steam ahead. Unlike fellow Fire signs Aries or Leo, who might say, "damn the consequences," the Archer simply doesn't think about them. In not doing so, she often ends up antagonizing everyone around. That's never her intention, but it won't make you feel any better when you're ready to kick her butt. The good news is that your Archer coworker is so kindhearted, cheerful, and well meaning that you won't stay angry at her for long.

Ruled by boundless Jupiter, Archers can have either a limitless supply of visionary ideas or an endless reserve of useless information. Astrology calls this sign the truth seeker of the universe, and that's why you'll rarely see an Archer sitting behind a desk all day. He's roaming the store, chatting with customers, hanging out in another department learning how widgets are made, or out of the office at a seminar.

Aries Fire is an inferno, and Leo Fire can be as harsh as the Sun. Sagittarius Fire, however, is warm and welcoming, like a crackling fireplace. A cinder might pop out onto your foot now and then, but without lasting damage. The main thing about having an Archer for a work buddy is that you're practically guaranteed that nothing will be dull—ever.

FAMOUS ADVENTUROUS ARCHERS

- Steven Spielberg, Oscar-winning filmmaker (December 18)
- Jon Stewart, comedian (November 28)
- Jake Gyllenhaal, actor (December 19)

SAGITTARIUS ON THE JOB

If you're going to kick authority in the teeth, you might as well use both feet.

KEITH RICHARDS (DECEMBER 18)

Working with an Archer is kind of like watching a three-ring circus. Your Gemini colleague can multitask like crazy, but your Sadge work buddy never sits still. Her calendar will be crammed with appointments, meetings, and workshops. Archers hate to miss a thing. Astrologically, her soul is on a quest for knowledge. Whether it's circulating through the company making friends with every other employee, checking out a customer's business, or visiting the home office in Europe, to a Sadge, the only way to learn is firsthand.

An enthusiastic, high-energy Sagittarius livens up the workplace with his contagious cheerfulness and sense of humor. When things look the bleakest, you can depend on him to either make a joke to relieve the tension or come up with an alternative plan that often saves the day.

Archers are known as hard-driving achievers; however, one reason your Sagittarius colleague often works on the weekends isn't entirely due to a willingness to take on extra responsibility. More often than not, he's trying to catch up from conducting his personal business, and probably a hefty social life, on company time.

You won't have to worry about making friends. Archers never know a stranger. She'll approach you as if you've known each other all your lives. This office pal is a whirlwind of information, ideas, and unselfish camaraderie.

Managing an Archer
Give Them a Long Leash

A Sagittarius needs to feel independent to thrive. Stick a footloose Archer in the farthest corner of the workplace, and the next time you check on him you'll find that he's disappeared. A bored Sagittarius won't wilt like Libra or start a second business on your time like Gemini. He'll simply go out and find himself a better job—either within the company, or, if that's not an option, he'll quit. Nothing can pin an Archer down.

Travel appeals to all Archers. If possible, put her in a situation where she can promote your company, either through local organizations or on business trips. She'll make a fabulous goodwill ambassador when you're thinking of merging or trying to win new clients in a competitive marketplace. If physically getting out of the workplace isn't possible, she'll excel as an internal go-to person for information about everything from how the copier works to the latest changes within your industry.

He's one of the zodiac's overachievers, and he's never satisfied with the status quo. He'll read every production manual and memorize industry benchmarks. He can quote federal regulations as easily as the company handbook. He'll produce a growth plan and supply the steps to achieve it. Let him be your resource person, and you'll always be a mile ahead of the competition.

Keep Them Enthused

As far as money's concerned, your Archer will expect fair pay for the job—and she'll know what that is, because this sign keeps up on issues such as average pay scales and fair-labor practices.

Sagittarius craves constant challenge. Toss him in the middle of a crisis, and he'll sort out the issues, pump up the staff with enthusiasm, and bring the opposing factions together into a cohesive team. Like Libra, the Archer is a good negotiator. The difference is that once the ground rules are in place, Sagittarius steps back. He treats his team as capable colleagues, not wussies who need micromanaging.

The Power of Positive Thinking author, Sagittarius Dale Carnegie, said, "Do the hard jobs first. The easy jobs will take care of themselves."

That's your Archer's philosophy, too. Don't waste him on a mundane job. Give him problems to unravel and new theories to test. He'll be in Archer heaven, and you'll be rolling in the dough.

Keep Them Grounded

An Archer can be engrossed in a project, yet overhear a conversation two desks away, make a mental note to follow up on a good idea, and have an outline on your desk before quitting time. Great asset, right? Yes—when he's not also covering the phone for an ill coworker, plus trying to teach another work pal a new computer program.

A Sagittarius coworker of mine knew everything from how big the Christmas bonus was to who dated whom. She was the first to volunteer to take on extra projects. Her suggestions frequently earned kudos from the VIPs. All was peachy until the day the boss handed her back a project with several important details missing.

Support your Archer's spirit of teamwork while keeping tabs on her. The worst habit your Sagittarius employee has is trying to help everyone else while speeding through her own work. This results in errors of omission. Keep her on track by always reviewing the finished product before you let her send it out. Give her candid feedback, and don't worry about sending her into an emotional tailspin like Watery Cancer or touchy Libra. Archers don't need coddling and appreciate constructive criticism.

Surviving Boss Archer
Know What You're Dealing With

I've had two Archer bosses, and both were bighearted, liberal, and cheerful. Each would roll up his or her sleeves and work with me to get the job done. So will yours. Of course, the flip side of that generous coin is that this might mean you're stuck boxing up electronic gizmos until midnight to ship to a client in Europe. Although she'll expect you to work hard, Boss

Archer also believes in fair play. Plus, she has a knack for knowing how much you can take before you start to crumble.

Unlike arrogant Leo or social-climbing Capricorn, Boss Archer couldn't care less whether he's the first millionaire on the block or if his name's listed in *Who's Who*. Oh, he likes money as much as the next guy. But what he loves is envisioning his next grand scheme on how to expand the corporation into six more countries or create a companywide cross-training program. The hiccup here is that sometimes he acts like a Macy's Thanksgiving Day balloon—full of hot air and always operating three stories above the crowd. Keeping this boss grounded with facts, time frames, and cost guidelines keeps you at the top of his most valued employee list.

Prepare for Chaos

Boss Archer's desk is usually overloaded with projects and reports. It's not that he doesn't delegate—your desk will be proof of that—it's that this boss doesn't know how to say no. Sagittarius is ruled by Jupiter, the supreme god of mythology. Unfortunately, when this all-knowing energy morphs into human form, he becomes Boss Catchall for every stray project around. Creating a routine by updating this boss when he first walks in the door each day will keep him on track and earn you his praise.

He'll want to cram in as much as possible in the morning so that he can sit in for his boss at an all-afternoon planning meeting. Or he'll sign up for every business conference around the country and be gone for a month. In doing so, he'll forget appointments or a hot item on his to-do list because he's been sidetracked by another big deal. Keep him connected with conference calls. Draft the project he needs and shoot it to him via e-mail so that he can tweak it and get it to his boss on time. Keeping this boss organized is a big job. If you can manage it, he'll think he can't get along without you.

SAGITTARIUS WORDS TO LIVE BY

"I'll do what I think is right and worry about it later."
—Ed Harris (November 28)

"The roughest roads often lead to the top."
—Christina Aguilera (December 18)

Watch Her Back

A Sagittarius boss is the most easygoing in the zodiac. She'll let you be as flexible as possible with your work schedule, be agreeable about long weekends, or be amenable when you want to leave early to get your hair done for a big date.

That said, this boss can have the same liberal attitude about her own job. She's not lazy; she's being as fair to herself as she is to you. The caveat is that her boss may or may not have the same perspective. That won't matter though, because Boss Archer doesn't always follow the rules.

Although some Archer bosses are scatterbrained spendthrifts who run amok with their company expense accounts, most are intensely dedicated and hardworking. Unless yours is the former, help her get a break now and then by covering for her when she's decided to get a massage versus attending another tiresome staff meeting.

Look at it this way: You've most likely hit the boss jackpot with an Archer. She'll fight for your job in tough times and argue on your behalf for a raise to match the extra responsibilities you've assumed. Should you or she leave the company, this boss will continue to be your friend and mentor. You can always talk openly without fear, and when you're in trouble, you can count on her support. Isn't that worth a little white lie?

Coping with a Sagittarius Coworker

Your Sagittarius colleague is open and candid. He's always willing to dispense advice should you need a shoulder to lean on. This office chum keeps his troubles to himself and rarely gets snappy. Show him that you appreciate him with a silly gift or a funny e-mail card. This dynamic coworker rarely asks for assistance. Earn his allegiance by offering to help when you see that he's overloaded.

Prepare for Friendly Mayhem

Working with a Sagittarius can be similar to standing in the middle of a whirlwind—simultaneously exhilarating and irritating. If her work is caught up, she won't hesitate to hop over to your area ready to download the latest juicy rumors. If you allow it, this coworker can chatter the afternoon away. Although she will notice if you're busy, she won't stop talking.

As do all Fire signs, the Archer assumes that you're an adult. So be one. You won't hurt her feelings if you tell her you don't have time to visit, and you don't have to qualify it with an invitation to lunch later as you would with some other signs. Archers aren't born without a take-offense gene, but it operates at such a low level that you'd have to deliberately try to hurt her feelings to activate it.

Keep Your Guard Up

It's a rare Sagittarius that will resort to backstabbing behavior. Like Aries, an Archer prefers to stab you in the front and watch the surprised look on your face.

Rotten Archers are usually loud, rude, and prone to trying to embarrass you in front of your peers or the boss. Unlike bad Leo, who wants to discredit your work, an Archer is out to make you look foolish or, worse, will disclose a personal tidbit in hopes of humiliating you.

He'll drop a bombshell (like you had an affair with the Xerox man) during coffee break, then bellow his horse laugh trying to act as if it's all a joke. Shrug your shoulders and grin. If you act like it's a joke, you'll diffuse the venom, and he'll look like what he is—a tactless clown.

If she's rivaling you for a promotion or after your job, the Archer, similar to Cancer, will try to buddy up. It's hard for this sign to cover her feelings, so you can tell when she's being insincere; her usually cheerful smile turns into a fixed grimace.

SAGITTARIUS CHEAP SHOTS

- Exhibits phony friendliness
- Wastes your time with gossip
- Spills personal stories

Learn to Love Them

It's easy to love an Archer. Most are open-minded, full of life, and always up for any kind of adventure, on or off the job.

What's nice about them is that nine out of ten don't have a mean bone in their bodies. Yes, they have tempers. Yes, they can get snippy, the same as we all can. But your Archer office mate is usually the one person you can count on to be consistent: He'll always help when you ask. He'll always work for the good of everyone. He'll always be a team player.

There will be times when you'll cringe from her blunt opinion or sting from one of her offhanded observations. However, she'll also be the first to gather money to send you flowers when you're sick, and she'll be at the head of the line to congratulate you on a success. You don't really have to watch your back around your average Archer, and in today's workplace, that's a rare gift.

IF YOU ARE A SAGITTARIUS

Work . . . is like getting on a train. Are you going sixty miles an hour, or is the train going sixty . . . and you're just sitting on it?

J. PAUL GETTY (NOVEMBER 15)

You're confident and hopeful. Your built-in optimism helps you see some opportunity in even the bleakest situation. You believe in treating everyone equally, and you rarely lose your temper, even if the boss is being a jerk or you get caught in a coworker's bitch attack. You're supportive of colleagues throughout the good and the bad.

So how can you take your career from mundane to marvelous?

Don't Get Sidetracked

You're a self-motivated person. You have big ideas and no fear about doing everything it takes to make them come true. You also believe there's no such thing as too much education.

However, because you want to know as much as possible about everything, you can scatter your energies, like Gemini, in trying to work toward multiple goals at once. The difference is that the Twin can quickly lose interest and drop a couple of tasks, while you stick with it no matter how long it takes. That's how you hurt your career. When you spend so much time trying to do it all, you leave yourself wide open to get passed over in favor of a more-focused, if less-educated, rival.

If you want to succeed, you have to train yourself to be more methodical. You're one of the quickest learners in the universe, and there isn't anything you can't accomplish in record time if you concentrate on sticking to one goal at a time.

Control Your Urge to Merge

Forget job jumping. You're one of the zodiac's major mattress hoppers. Along with Aries, Gemini, and Libra, the terms workplace and playhouse can be synonymous to some of you Archers. Using your charisma to charm a surly customer is one thing, but using the company as your exclusive Club Bed is something else.

Your zodiac symbol is the mythological half man, half beast centaur, who hunted his prey with a bow and arrow. All too often the target of you human versions is revolving-door romance.

Having a boy- or girlfriend at work is totally acceptable today. However, your penchant for serial dating your way through the company can make you look shallow and easy. If you want to get more than a rep as the company gigolo, stick to company business at work and practice your monkey business on your own time.

TIPS FOR SUCCESS

- Stick to one goal at a time
- Put your hormones on hold on company time
- Watch your own back

Bash a Backstabber

Despite your reputation as a hard-driving, hard-as-nails go-getter, you're one of the most naive signs in the zodiac. Because you meet life head on and honestly, you think that everyone else is honest, too. That's why you are totally shocked when someone you thought was a trusted colleague tries to discredit you behind your back.

Although your first instinct might be to yell loud enough for the entire office to hear, think of the consequences for you. Take the betrayer aside and unleash your wrath in private. Most people are not used to being called out, but thanks to your Jupiter-fueled spirit, you have zero trouble making the perp face up to his or her bad behavior.

Protect yourself by being wise about whom you confide in. You don't have to stifle your friendly nature, but being more observant about other people's behavior can help you avoid getting hurt.

FROM FED UP TO FIRED UP

If you're waiting for the right moment, others who are not will take over.

WOODY ALLEN (DECEMBER 1)

You fight to get your proposal presented, present a tough case for a midyear raise, and won't hesitate to back up a pal who's been the target of untrue rumors. You can have great ideas on how to streamline a time-consuming project or to make your workplace run more efficiently. Your challenge is to be aware of how your brash, sometimes ballsy, behavior affects those around you.

Watch Your Mouth

One of your worst habits is unintentionally offending a colleague with a thoughtless remark. Your worst habit is acting clueless while deliberately pissing him off.

Sometimes beneath that harmless smile of yours lurks the snarky desire to drop a zinger just to see what reaction you get. You also aren't quite as naive as others assume, so you can use your caustic humor as public payback. This is fine if you intend to remain just another working slob until Social Security kicks in. But if you want to get ahead, get control of yourself.

Stopping the deliberate barbs is easy. Becoming aware of the unconscious bombshells you drop takes practice. Following the old saying "*Make sure your brain is in gear before setting your mouth in motion*" is something you should learn. One way is to deliberately speak slower. When you think for a few seconds first, you'll soon be able to stifle an involuntary insult. When you control what you say, you'll come across as professional and powerful. When that happens, you'll take a giant leap forward.

Know When to Quit

For a Fire sign, you can hang on to a so-so job almost as long as a security-loving Taurus. You don't fear change; you have a laid-back side that kicks in when you get into a comfort-zone combination of just enough money and just enough motion. Transferring within your company can satisfy your need to learn new things, and getting steady raises or the occasional bump in responsibility can be enough incentive to prevent you from seeking a top-notch job.

Giving you advice to make the rounds of headhunters, to read the trade journals for possibilities, or to check the want ads is useless. You know that already, and you won't make a move until you're ready. Sooner or later, if you're truly interested in moving up, you'll know it's time to go. That's when your vast network of professional acquaintances pays off. Chances are you'll send one group e-mail, and within a couple of days you'll be bombarded with possibilities.

Ace an Interview

Your jam-packed résumé and down-to-earth personality impress the toughest interviewer. Your impressive knowledge of the company you're applying to boosts you to the head of the applicant line. But you have two habits that can get you demoted from top choice to no-way-in-hell.

Like all Fire signs, when you're nervous, you get loud. In your case, your cheerful and constant chuckle morphs into an ear-splitting shriek if you're a woman or horse-laugh guffaw if you're a guy. You also get off track by digressing into a circuitous tale about everything that's ever happened in your professional life, which makes you sound more boring than the most minutiae-blathering Virgo. You think you're making headway, but the interviewer is wondering what she can find to stuff in her ears.

Help calm your nerves by parking a few blocks away and walk to your interview. If the weather's bad, arrive early and sit in your car for a few minutes, listening to the rain or watching the snow fall. Being outside is a sure way to help you to relax. As for curbing your motormouth, make a list of the important points you want to make and glance at it now and then to stay on track.

Sagittarius-Friendly Careers

Astrology puts religion, philosophy, and publishing at the top of your career list. You have the intellect and talent to tackle any one of these or any profession you choose. Where you'll thrive is in a job that allows you the freedom to pursue your ideas and learn new things.

Travel Guide

What better way to satisfy both your soul-deep wanderlust and curiosity about the wonders of the world than to travel around the globe with a captive audience and get paid for it?

College Professor

Expounding on the mysteries of the universe or inspiring your students to broaden their outlook by studying abroad fits your needs to impart knowledge and make an impact on the world.

Thrill Seeker

Whether you're on a mission to ride every megacoaster in the world and write a memoir of the experience, or you're determined to trek to the top of the Himalayas in search of a yeti, having a life of reckless adventure is your secret dream.

Outdoorsperson

Whether you're a mountain climber, a forest ranger, or a nature photographer, turning your love of the outdoors into a lucrative career is a natural for you.

Talk-Show Host

Interviewing celebrities on TV appeals to your curiosity about human nature, and discussing the latest UFO sightings or other unexplained phenomena on a midnight radio show satisfies your urge to philosophize. Bonus: Here's where your barbed tongue can make you a star.

CHAPTER ELEVEN

Capricorn

December 22–January 19

Element:	Earth
Quality:	Cardinal
Symbol:	The Goat
Ruler:	Saturn
Key word:	Ambitious
Work-a-tude:	Stick to business.

INSTANT INSIGHTS

Courage is found in unlikely places.

J. R. R. Tolkien (January 3)

Ambitiously as sure-footed as his symbol, the nimble mountain goat, a Capricorn never stops until he reaches a goal. Astrology labels him as industrious, disciplined, and coolly efficient. You can also tag him as inflexible, pessimistic, and bossy.

Feminine Cardinal Capricorn lives in the Tenth House of career and public recognition. This is the pad that deals with fame and reputation. A go-getting Aries wants to be first, but the determined Goat wants to be the best. Ruled by tradition-loving, sometimes surly, Saturn, your Capricorn coworker can belong to the "*if it ain't broke, don't fix it*" school of business. Unlike Aquarius, who believes everything can stand improvement, most cautious Goats don't like to tamper with a tried-and-true system—even if it's outdated. As a Feminine sign, the Goat usually won't immediately take offense, as a head-butting Masculine Ram might. She prefers to find a way to work around conflict, much like her symbol picks its way through the boulders on its climb up a mountain. Like Virgo, no can be the first word out of her mouth. Unless it's her idea, a Goat resists change.

Capricorns also make things happen. You won't see this office chum waste time on trivial tasks, and you won't hear him whine about being overworked. The combination of his Earth nature and serious Saturn-ruled character gives him a realistic, if grim, attitude about what it takes to succeed. Your Capricorn coworker keeps his feet on the ground and eyes on the finish line. He won't stop until he gets what he's after. The Goat is perfectly willing to work seven days a week for months or years to reach a goal.

This coworker's sensible, straightforward advice can help you get organized and manage your time. You can also depend on his word. If he says he'll be at your desk at 10:00 a.m. to help with a project, he will.

FAMOUS TOP-OF-THE-HEAP GOATS

- Michelle Obama, First Lady of the United States (January 17)
- Conrad Hilton Sr., founder of the Hilton Hotel chain (December 25)
- Nicolas Cage, actor (January 7)

Cardinal Air Libra guides with negotiation. She sees both side of an issue and will try to do the best for both parties. Cardinal Fire Aries commands by intimidation. He can make threats to get his way. Cardinal Water Cancer controls with manipulation. She maneuvers behind the scenes to get the upper hand. Cardinal Earth Capricorn, however, leads by determination. He lets nothing stop him. His goal is the only goal.

CAPRICORN ON THE JOB

I just wanted to get famous. All the rest is hogwash.

ANTHONY HOPKINS (DECEMBER 31)

Some other signs may spend the day looking for ways to avoid work, but savvy Capricorn is busy making herself indispensable by learning the ropes from the bottom up.

The quiet Goat has a dry, wickedly funny sense of humor. Just when you think this colleague is the shy, retiring type, he'll catch you off guard and crack you up with a straight-faced dig or wry observation. As playful as any other sign off the job, this coworker is all business at work. He won't waste time on personal calls or goof off when business is slow.

This isn't the office chum to go whining to when you're having a bad day. Her matter-of-fact advice (get over it or get out), although well meant, can make you think she's hard-hearted. Not true. She's a sympathetic listener. However, emotional scenes can make this reserved sign uncomfortable. She won't wear her heart on her sleeve, but she will help you find a practical solution to your problem.

Like Scorpio, she can be suspicious of your motives, so don't expect her to warm up too fast. Capricorn is the sign of reciprocation, so the best way to earn her respect and friendship is to be as dependable as she is. If you offer help, don't flake on her. Paying back her assistance with support of your own earns the diligent Goat's respect.

Managing a Capricorn
Give Them Responsibility

From bus boy to assistant manager to mail clerk, a practical Goat will take any entry-level job to get his foot in the door when he wants to work for you. He has one intention: to use that as the first stepping stone in his climb up Career Mountain. As do fellow Earth signs Virgo and Taurus, your Goat needs to feel useful and that he's making a solid contribution. Unlike them, he's never comfortable with the status quo. He needs to keep moving forward.

Expecting a Capricorn to slog through the same routine day after day is as unrealistic as thinking that you can get a Virgo to rush. The more responsibility you give your Goat, the better she'll perform. This diligent employee can handle as much work as a Taurus, manage people as well as a Leo, and understand the inner workings of the company better than a Sagittarius. She's conscientious, thorough, and respectful.

Give her progressively bigger tasks to accomplish and more complicated issues to figure out. Encourage her to apply for a promotion and reward her with fair and steady raises. Your Capricorn is determined to succeed, and when she does, so will business.

Keep Them Enthused

Astrology calls Capricorn the manager of the zodiac. Although plenty of them are bosses, the literal translation is that a Goat is good at giving direction, saving time, and seeing that policies are carried out or procedures are correctly followed. His know-how and knowledge of day-to-day operations give him the ability to cut through the red tape to get problems solved.

Make her the leader of a performance improvement team and watch how quickly error rates drop in her department. Let her organize the staff work schedules to maximize production and minimize overtime. She has a nose for sniffing out time- or money-wasting inefficiencies.

Trust him with an important task and let him handle it in his own way. He might take a little more time to complete it, but you can bet he'll find a flaw to fix or discover an accounting error that could have cost prof-

its. He might not be a brainstorming whiz like an Aquarius or Gemini, but a Goat is made to manage daily activities. Turn him loose with a budget and the authority to make a few changes, and you'll be amazed at how fast your bottom line moves from marginal to mega profit.

Beware the Head Butting

Ninety-five percent of the time, a Capricorn will do anything to please you because she wants to be your best performer. The other 5 percent will be spent resisting changes and questioning new procedures. Being ruled by conventional Saturn makes the Goat's motto: "That's the way we've always done it."

You'll have to be tough to get her to change. Give her the directive and a time frame to get it done. No questions asked; no compromise. Be professional and kind, however. Remember, the Goat is a Feminine sign and sensitive despite her sometimes gruff exterior. She respects authority. Once she sees that you're serious, she'll tackle the change with the same energy she used to bitch at you, and then she'll become the expert whom everyone else can go to for help.

Surviving Boss Goat

Know What You're Dealing With

Unless you're serious about doing the very best you can every minute of every day, don't even consider working for a Capricorn. Less volatile but more demanding than an Aries, Boss Goat is the hardest-driving boss in the zodiac. She gives 110 percent to her job and will expect the same from you. She's neither as title conscious as a Leo nor as power hungry as a Scorpio. The Goat craves prestige. She wants the respect of both her peers and the VIPs. To earn it, she'll be the first one on the job in the morning and the last to leave at night.

Her personality swings from cool but professional to Cruella De Vil in a business suit. She would fire her mother if she thought Mom wasn't pulling her weight. Let that be a warning.

Like Aries, Boss Goat sees you as a reflection of him. But in addition to wanting you to present a stylish appearance, he'll expect you to share his work ethic. Never let this boss catch you talking on the phone or surfing the Internet. If you waste the time he's paying you to work, you can bet the next place you'll be filing your fingernails is in the unemployment line.

So how do you become indispensable to this demanding boss?

Be Resilient

With formidable Saturn as his ruler, Boss Goat can be almost as moody as a Crab, nitpick the tiniest details better than a Libra, and be as intimidating as a Ram.

Boss Goat periodically gets melancholy. Instead of assuming that things will always work out, like Sagittarius, Capricorn can look at life from a pessimistic viewpoint. When that happens, she'll withdraw. Classic movie star Marlene Dietrich, a Capricorn, said, "I want to be alone." When she feels down, so does a Goat. She'll have minimal contact with you and the rest of the staff. Respect her space and handle as many issues that pop up as you can. Also use the respite to get your work caught up, because when the gloom lifts, she'll be recharged and twice as demanding.

If you're the type who needs to have your head patted multiple times a day or expects any praise on a regular basis, you're in for a rude awakening. Boss Goat's viewpoint is that your reward is the paycheck you get each week. Go above and beyond by landing an unexpected million-dollar deal or snagging an exclusive client, and he'll pat your back. He never gushes over anything, but the surprise you get with a profit-minded Goat is that you'll probably find two tickets for a weekend cruise or a gift certificate to the best restaurant in town on your desk the next morning.

CAPRICORN WORDS TO LIVE BY

"Never listen to other people's expectations. You should live your own life and live up to your own expectations."
—Tiger Woods (December 30)

"Life opens up opportunities for you, and you either take them or are afraid to take them."
—Jim Carrey (January 17)

Expect to Be under Surveillance

Boss Goat is one of the micromanagers of the zodiac. He'll stand over your shoulder while you sort the day's receipts, spot-check your routine work, or drop in unexpectedly to see if you're slacking off.

Don't take it personally. Capricorn thinks that wasting time is a sin, and he'll spend part of each day making the rounds to see that everything in his domain is clicking along as efficiently as possible.

Keep your eye on her, too. Not her work, but her health. When the pressure's on, a Capricorn boss can forget to eat. Don't hover. Do offer to bring her back a sandwich when you go to lunch or suggest that she take a walk. Fresh air in any weather renews a Goat's energy.

Despite his reputation for being a hard-ass, this boss will be one of the first to advise you to learn everything you can about your job, encourage you to try for a promotion, and give you a glowing recommendation. All you have to do is do your job.

Coping with a Capricorn Coworker

Your Capricorn colleague is friendly, full of handy information, and helpful. She's also emotionally distant, but not because she's a snob, as sometimes described. She doesn't need an entourage of fans as Leo might or your shoulder to cry on as Cancer can. The Goat is the true loner of the zodiac. Underneath her aloof exterior, she's sensitive and as full of secret dreams as anyone.

Keep It Real

If you're teamed with a Goat on a project, make sure to pull your weight. This colleague doesn't crumble under pressure and won't hesitate to tell you she can do it alone if she thinks you're getting frazzled.

Goats can be as blunt with criticism as Scorpio and as opinionated as Aquarius. But unlike these signs, she can take it as good as she dishes it out. If she's on your case about something, stand up to her. She's tough, feisty, and will try to run the show. Earn her respect by being able to butt heads once in a while without either losing your temper or letting her get the upper hand.

Capricorns can't be bothered with playing head games. Oh, she's not above sucking up to a VIP to further her career or attending a boring business event to widen her professional network. It's the day-to-day gossip that she avoids. This office chum is focused on getting ahead, so don't try to impress her with a juicy tidbit unless it's an insider tip that will boost her career.

Off the clock, she's fun and up for anything. Invite her to grab an early dinner after work or to hit a white sale at the nearest outlet center. Most Capricorns have a small circle of close friends. Become one of them by following her motto: "Work hard, play harder."

Keep Your Guard Up

The first rule to learn about a Capricorn is that you can't intimidate him—but a bad one will use any means possible to try to intimidate you. He'll sting you with a petty remark and tell you to your face you're not qualified to do your current job, let alone apply for a promotion. Think of a real goat crashing headlong into its opponent. This is how the human version operates.

Because of the sign's Feminine nature, the Goat is just as apt to use underhanded methods, such as being nice to your face and telling the boss you're an idiot behind your back. Some have the nasty habit of waiting until things cool down, then sabotaging a project or backing out of an offer to help that leaves you in a mess at the last minute.

The best way to handle this rotten coworker is to be just as tough. Don't push first. However, if she makes a snide remark in the break room, bite back with one of your own. Don't put yourself in a situation where you have to depend on her, even if she appears to be friendly. Act like a Goat yourself and tell her, "No thanks. I can handle it."

CAPRICORN CHEAP SHOTS

- Exacts sly revenge when you least expect it
- Is openly confrontational
- Acts two-faced

Learn to Love Them

Your Capricorn coworker might be all business on the outside, but inside, she's vulnerable and sensitive. Bitching about others being whiny or indecisive is her defense system. Her repressive, Saturn-ruled character gives her the built-in belief that any sign of weakness is also a sign of failure.

Yes, she's headstrong and bossy. She can be standoffish and so outspoken that your ears will burn. However, no other office mate will understand your need to succeed better or be more willing to help you brainstorm a plan of action.

He also has a deep compassion for an underdog. I worked with a Capricorn VIP who was always ready to offer assistance in a crisis, money for a good cause, or his personal time to a staff member who needed help.

Your Capricorn office pal will work beside you all day and party with you all night. She's a pro at whatever she does and won't expect you to pick up her slack. It takes time to win her friendship, but if you look beneath the surface and offer her a chance to open up her real feelings, you'll find a warmhearted pal who will work as hard at your friendship as she does at her job.

IF YOU ARE A CAPRICORN

Ambition is a dream with a V-8 engine.

ELVIS PRESLEY (JANUARY 8)

Your boss depends on you. Your coworkers know they can count on you. You're strong, act self-assured even when you aren't, and won't stop until you reach the top.

How then can you get there without driving either yourself or everyone around you to distraction?

Loosen Up

You're the workaholic of the zodiac. Whether you're selling beauty products from home or saving lives in the operating room, you have one aim— to be the best at what you do.

The downside of this admirable trait is that in trying to do it all, you alternate between manic mode and periods of depression where you totally turn off. Plus, if you do convince yourself to drop everything to have fun with your pals, you're guilty about leaving any loose ends at work.

You can get so caught up in your job that you aren't aware of your mood until it's too late. What you must do is learn to recognize the signs of a downswing before it hits. Maybe every comment you hear irritates you. Maybe you feel too tired to get out of bed. When you pay attention, you can help to rescue yourself with a day off, a spa visit, or a long weekend.

Use your organizational skills to schedule frequent social events (no shop talk allowed) where you can relax. Get a hobby. Learn to paint or take a history class. Getting lost in a leisure pursuit clears your mind and reduces stress.

You're smart about what you want in life, so don't foolishly risk your emotional or physical health by trying to do it all, all the time.

Don't Expect the Worst

Astrology paints you as the sign that never gives up. You don't, but you lean toward the glass-half-empty philosophy of life. While you rarely verbalize your fears, worrying about what might happen can stop you in your sure-footed tracks.

You put off getting started because you think up roadblocks that might prevent you from reaching a goal. In the time it takes you to mull over the ten or twenty things that could go wrong, someone else has jumped three rungs ahead of you on the career ladder.

"Attitude is everything" isn't just an empty cliché. It's been proven that the thoughts and feelings we project attract like ones. Try to stay aware of the times you put out negative vibes. "If I got the promotion, I'd probably just get hit by a bus anyway" is no way to approach a potentially career-boosting move. Remember, you are a mountain goat. There isn't an obstacle you can't overcome or a roadblock you can't sidestep as long as you make up your mind to do it.

TIPS FOR SUCCESS

- Keep a positive attitude
- Be aware of your caustic tongue
- Schedule time-outs so you don't burn out

Get Your Nose out of the Air

Whether you mean to or not, you often come across as an aloof, social-climbing snob. Although you're always nice to the boss (she signs the checks), VIPs in general (insider tips), and powerful community figures (possible mentors), you have a habit of looking right through your peers or coworkers who are further down the ladder. This gives you the rep as someone who's only friendly to people who have something to offer.

Maybe that's true, but it's not smart. The stock boy you snub today could be the boss's nephew who becomes your supervisor next month. The colleague you bitch out for publicly disagreeing with your latest brainstorm could be the one who gets handed a top assignment and decides to leave you off her team.

Remember the old cliché, "What goes around, comes around." Courtesy doesn't cost a cent, but the value you reap from being pleasant to everyone you see can be priceless.

FROM FED UP TO FIRED UP

I say luck is when an opportunity comes along and you're prepared for it.

DENZEL WASHINGTON (DECEMBER 28)

You're diligent, organized, and honest. You can handle anything on or off the job, and you know the value of both time and money. You inspire trust in your boss, coworkers, and customers. Your struggle is to learn that you can't do it alone.

Stop Doing It the Hard Way

You subscribe to the *"no pain, no gain"* philosophy of life. The trouble is that you often bring much of your pain on yourself. You can be so obstinate that you alienate your coworkers with your refusal to see any viewpoint but your own.

Put you on a team, and in five minutes you're giving directives and handing out solutions without bothering to get anyone else's input. Assign you to work with a colleague on a project, and you immediately relegate her to your assistant while closing your mind to her suggestions. Collaboration might be a dirty word to you, but without it, your climb to the top is going to take twice as long. Or worse, you might not make it because you've trampled so many people trying to climb the ladder that they gang up to ensure you fall off. Demanding your way or automatically assuming that you know more than the next guy is arrogant. Bossing your peers around is a sure way to get stabbed in the back.

As a Cardinal sign, you like to think that you know best. However, the real test of leadership is valuing the input and opinions of your colleagues.

Know When to Quit

You might be known as steadfast and patient, but you lean toward the job-hopping bunch of the zodiac. This is because in trying to get ahead, you frequently end up bumping heads. Then you get disgusted because you're not getting your way and walk out.

You might get more responsibility, then balk because you aren't given free reign over your job. Or you're offended because the boss won't promote you as fast as you think you should be. You're enthused one day, frustrated the next, and sending out your résumé the day after that.

You understand that it takes time to get ahead. However, also understanding that your timetable and the boss's rarely coincide can go a long way toward saving you from committing career suicide. Ask your boss how or if you can fast-track your next promotion. Some companies have a rule against applying for a promotion within a certain time frame after you've been hired. Learn your options and evaluate them. Then you can make a smart choice instead of wasting time leaping from one dead-end job to another.

Ace an Interview

Your impeccable appearance and cool-under-fire personality make a fabulous first impression. Your no-nonsense approach to answering the toughest questions makes a positive impact on the person asking them. You can shoot yourself in the foot, however, by appearing overconfident.

Describing the technique you used to save your last company money is one thing, but bragging that you saved the boss's butt because you were so much smarter is conceited and will land you on the five-minute-interview list of losers.

The danger is that you don't always know when you're coming across as smug. You think you're validating that you're brainy and not afraid to assume responsibility, but the interviewer thinks you're a pretentious dolt.

Consider several practice runs with a friend first. Stick to the facts of how you accomplished a complicated task. Don't put your former colleagues, boss, or company down. If you stay aware of what you're saying, there isn't any interviewer you can't amaze.

Capricorn-Friendly Careers

Astrology paints you as serious, focused, and disciplined. Often-listed careers for you include banker, economist, or administrator. That doesn't mean you can't be a fabulous salesperson or creative artist, however. On the contrary, you'll succeed precisely because of your diligence and careful planning.

The following are several career possibilities.

Jeweler

Your eye for spotting the perfect stone and flair for creating a one-of-a-kind designer piece that perfectly suits your client's taste and style keeps you in demand.

Operations Manager
Whether you're running your own day spa or are the concierge of a five-star hotel, you have no trouble keeping on top of the hundreds of details that keep the business humming.

Career Counselor
Helping people find their direction in life and set a timetable to achieve their goals appeals to you. Bonus: Here's your chance to tell people what's good for them and get paid for it.

Engineer / Architect
Whether building bridges or creating luxury homes, you have an eye for precision, a talent for cutting costs without sacrificing quality, and a sense of style that can propel you the top of the most-sought-after designer list.

Restoration Expert
Restoring antique furniture to its original beauty or spending months cleaning and repairing a priceless piece of art appeals to your sense of tradition and love of the past.

CHAPTER TWELVE

Aquarius

January 20–February 18

Element:	Air
Quality:	Fixed
Symbol:	The Water Bearer
Ruler:	Uranus
Key word:	Analytical
Work-a-tude:	I'll get back to you on that.

INSTANT INSIGHTS

Sometimes I've believed as many as six impossible things before breakfast.

LEWIS CARROLL (JANUARY 27)

Masculine Fixed Air Aquarius is the original freethinker of the universe. Living in the Eleventh House of friends, group associations, and wishes, Aquarius is sincere, unbiased, and cooperative. That is, when he's not being disruptive, radical, and controlling.

Uranus, the planet of innovation, revolution, and humanity, rules the Water Bearer. Your Aquarius colleague is concerned with how to make things better for everyone. From fine-tuning your company distribution system to devising a plan to more efficiently feed the homeless, he's forever tearing apart the status quo and trying to find a way to improve it. Some of his ideas might seem quirky or even weird, but to him it's the natural way his mind works.

His symbol, the Water Bearer, is portrayed as either a man or a woman pouring water from a large jar. This is the reason for the common misconception that airy Aquarius is a Water sign. However, the "water" he's giving to mankind is metaphorical knowledge—the fountain of endless wisdom. The hitch in this humanitarian ideal is that, when he's on a roll, a Water Bearer can talk longer and faster than Gemini and Sagittarius combined.

Whether he's a cab driver, the cable guy, or your friendly dentist, your Aquarius coworker has strong opinions about everything. He won't hesitate to discuss any subject under the sun, and whether he's a high-school dropout or has a Ph.D., he's an interesting combination of intellectual and oddball.

Aquarius is the most nonjudgmental sign in the zodiac. She doesn't care if you're employee of the month or on probation for chronic tardiness—her opinion of you won't be based on anything but how you and she mesh. She has a variety of friends from all walks of life. She might be curious to hear the latest gossip, but unlike other signs, the Water Bearer will rarely start or spread a rumor. She isn't interested in putting people down.

Fixed Fire Leo wants to rule his world. Fixed Earth Taurus wants to protect his world. Fixed Water Scorpio wants to control his world. Fixed Air Aquarius, however, wants to make his world, and yours, a better place.

FAMOUS AQUARIUS INDIVIDUALISTS

- Abraham Lincoln, the sixteenth president of the United States (February 12)
- John Grisham, best-selling author (February 8)
- Matt Groening, creator of *The Simpsons* (February 15)

AQUARIUS ON THE JOB

Real integrity is doing the right thing knowing that nobody's going to know whether you did it or not.

OPRAH WINFREY (JANUARY 29)

Working with a Water Bearer is interesting because, to paraphrase fictional character Forrest Gump, you never know *whom* you're going to get. One day he'll keep to himself and not speak to anyone, and the next day he'll storm in ranting about how the company's wasting water by running the sprinklers on a cloudy day. The day after that, he'll come up with an ingeniously simple way to solve a dilemma he overheard the secretary in a different department discussing at lunch.

No, he isn't dual natured like the Twin and Fish. His Uranus-ruled brain is full of ideas, all traveling at the speed of light. His Water Bearer symbol compels him to download them to anyone within earshot, and his Masculine assertiveness can make him (or her) short tempered when he perceives an injustice.

Because of his Fixed Air character, the Water Bearer isn't exactly a team player. He believes his ideas are best and can get as stubborn as any Taurus about changing them. That said, he has the rational ability to agree to compromise if everyone else disagrees with him. That's professional and in the spirit of the collective good. However, he'll still think his way is the best way.

Your Aquarius office chum is unpredictable, has a quirky sense of humor, and has a slightly skewed perspective on life. She's one of the easiest signs to make friends with, but what's hard is trying to keep up with her.

Managing a Water Bearer
Give Them Freedom

Your Aquarius employee won't care whether he has a window office or a cubicle in the back of the building, as long as it's his own space. Box him within a rigid company policy or demand that he adhere to a narrow set of rules, and he'll disappear faster than a Leo chasing a get-rich-quick scheme. The Water Bearer values personal freedom above anything. If possible, let him work flexible hours or take a midweek break and make up the time on the weekend.

He's an innovative thinker. Hand him a challenging assignment, then step away while he puts his original spin on it. Aquarius is great at assimilating facts and then spitting out solutions. It will probably be unusual, but it will work.

Like Gemini, the Water Bearer enjoys variety. The difference is that she's happiest working on complex issues, while the Twin likes to multitask simpler ones. Keep your Aquarius thriving with flexible working conditions and frequent challenges, and he'll help you keep your business flourishing.

Keep Them Enthused

The Water Bearer's attitude toward work is as unconventional as her belief system. This is the employee who'll happily work a rotating shift, job-share, or be your fill-in person.

Your Aquarius likes people. Thanks to her Eleventh House character that's based on friendship and the good of the group versus the individual, she has a natural talent for not getting caught up in others' emotional issues. Let her teach a conflict-resolution workshop or put her on an employee task force to develop a stress-reduction program. Her novel ideas can produce fun and original techniques.

She hates routine as much as any Sagittarius and is as curious as Gemini. The Water Bearer wants to know everything about the company. However, what's most important to her is getting to know everything about her coworkers. If possible, let her cross-train across a variety of departments. Because she views the company as one entity instead of a bunch of separate areas, she'll see how you can rearrange duties and concentrate tasks to streamline operations across the business.

Letting your Aquarius roam through the company is better than hiring a team of efficiency experts. He'll discover the holes in a process or procedure and find original ways to save money.

Beware the Negative Critic

A nasty habit some Aquarians have is appointing themselves class monitor over their coworkers, then bombarding you with criticisms. This can be anything from allusions to your slipshod management style to jealously attacking a more popular coworker. Maybe the hotshot Leo's just landed a big contract, or the chic Capricorn is getting more compliments on her poise under pressure, or the whole crew is too noisy.

When an average Water Bearer gets this critical, you can be sure that he's unhappy either in his personal or professional life. If he's a good employee and you don't want to lose him, sit him down and carefully listen to his concerns. Maybe there's a real issue in the litany he spews. Probing a bit deeper can help him to vent his stress. Whether or not it's something you can control, being willing to objectively hear him out can help to put him back on an even keel.

Surviving Boss Water Bearer

Know What You're Dealing With

An Aquarius boss with a conventional routine is as rare as a Leo boss with a low profile. Boss Water Bearer approaches both life and work from an off-

beat perspective. Innovative, nonjudgmental, and open-minded, this boss will not only appreciate your input, he'll expect it. That's the good news.

The bad news is that she can also be stubborn and controlling. As all Fixed signs, Boss Water Bearer thinks her way is the only way. The difference is that she'll happily share her ideas and ask your opinion in what she believes is a true, democratic fashion. Unfortunately, if you dare to disagree, she can turn into a pompous windbag hammering you with a dozen reasons why she's right. It's the irony of her Uranus-ruled character.

However, most of the time this boss is fair and impartial. He won't spend much time in his office and has no desire to hang over your shoulder spying on you. He won't micromanage the staff, and he usually won't care how you set up your schedule as long as the bases are covered.

He'll expect you to treat everyone at work fairly and impartially. He'll expect you to treat his smallest customer with the same deference and respect as you would the million-dollar one. An Aquarius boss strives for equality. Show him you're as unbiased and concerned for the well-being of the people around you as he is, and you'll win his respect.

Stay on the Cutting Edge

Both Aquarius and Pisces live in their heads as much as they live in the real world. They both dream of a universal ideal. The difference is that while the Fish can falter within a tight business structure and often does better working independently, the Water Bearer loves introducing (or forcing) new ideas into the establishment. She loves to shake things up.

Whether you're the cook in his diner or one of the architects in his building design firm, stay on top of the latest avant garde developments within your industry. Read the trade journals, network, and search the Internet. Keep this boss clued in, especially of those futuristic ideas that aren't reality yet or trends in other countries that haven't hit the home market.

Use your imagination, too. Of all the bosses in the zodiac, this is the one who won't think your most eccentric ideas are off track or out-of-bounds. They might not work, but progressive thinking is what he's all about. Keep him informed, feed his imagination with your original ideas, and brainstorm with him, and he'll keep you at the top of his team.

AQUARIUS WORDS TO LIVE BY

"If you don't have enemies, you don't have character."
—Paul Newman (January 26)

"Everything comes to he who hustles while he waits."
—Thomas Edison (February 11)

Dump Your Schedule

If you're a routine-loving Taurus or an order-craving Virgo, you might want to think twice before accepting a job as the sidekick of Boss Water Bearer. Aquarius is the most routine-loathing sign in the zodiac.

That doesn't mean she can't work within the business world. It means that, unlike Boss Crab, who likes to work from her office, or Boss Bull, who holds regular staff meetings, Boss Water Bearer has a hit-and-run style. She'll call a staff meeting the minute she walks in one day and decide to fly to China for a firsthand look at a new product the next. She'll forget an appointment because she got sidetracked brainstorming with a colleague in a different department, or she'll take an unscheduled day off.

You'll have to juggle her schedule, track her down, and keep her informed of what's happening while she's gone. Stay prepared by having your work caught up at all times. She might drop by at 10:00 p.m. to sign letters or come in at 5:00 a.m. to go through her in-box. But despite her irregular hours and seemingly haphazard approach, Boss Water Bearer has an uncanny knack for staying on top of everything.

Working for a Water Bearer can be disruptive and sometimes frustrating. You'll have to get used to dropping everything to work on his latest brainstorm or pulling together a state-of-the-art presentation before lunch. But you'll never have to worry about watching the clock, because time flies in this boss's world.

Coping with a Water Bearer Coworker

A Water Bearer coworker is interested in everything, from a distance. She'll rarely play office politics or join in the latest gossip. She's friendly with everyone, generous, and is usually an expert at what she does.

Don't Butt In

I had an Aquarius coworker whose favorite phrase was, "What do you think?" She wasn't trying to get me to make all the decisions; she was interested in what I had to say. So is your Water Bearer work pal. The caveat is that she doesn't like receiving unsolicited advice. You can offer to help, but don't get pushy about it.

She's usually quiet and keeps to herself, which can give her the reputation of being standoffish. Not true. This office pal respects your space and gives you the benefit of the doubt that if you need help, you'll ask. If you do, that's another story. She'll review it, think about it for a while, and then usually come up with at least one improvement.

He's the same way about his, or your, personal life. Superficial chatting is fine, but like Scorpio, the Water Bearer likes his privacy, and he won't pry into yours.

Water Bearers need emotional space. On the surface, he's friendly with everyone. He'll do lunch, happy hour, or contribute to a spring potluck. But he has a small, tight circle of close pals. Making casual friends is easy. Getting on his A-list will take patience, but it's worth the wait.

Keep Your Guard Up

Anytime things aren't going the way an Aquarian wants, he'll try to manipulate the action in his favor. If he wants A, and you want B, he'll present you with alternative C, based on your A idea but skewed so badly that B wins. Confused? That's the idea.

This is another colleague who will rarely try to actually steal your job. Usually when an Aquarius goes bad it's because he's trying to take control. He can get pushy about offering you advice or decide that he doesn't want to work with you because you weren't impressed by his latest wild idea or crazy scheme.

If she refuses to work with you, leave that issue up to the boss. If she gets pushy, be professional but ignore her. Don't make an excuse and don't bother trying to debate. When an Aquarius is on a rant, her Fixed Air turns into a verbal tornado. Thinking that you can prove your point by arguing with one will only make you hoarse. She doesn't want to negotiate; she wants to overwhelm you with her supposed superiority. Do your own thing and ignore her tirades. Silence is the best way to knock the wind out of an overbearing Aquarian.

AQUARIUS CHEAP SHOTS

- Deliberately confuses an issue
- Tries to take over
- Rants about you to anyone within earshot

Learn to Love Them

Your Water Bearer colleague is an eclectic mix of quirky personality traits, near-genius brainstorms, and sudden memory lapses. One day she's in your face trying to get you to join her latest cause, and the next she can't remember your name, or hers. She's full of lightbulb moments and will bombard you with each one. But she's just as enthusiastic about hearing yours.

He can be temperamental and impatient, but he's rarely deliberately mean-spirited. He also loves challenges and has a generous heart. He'll be first to sit down and help you unravel a complex problem. He's not always a team player, yet he works for the common good of the company.

Aquarius is, as the saying goes, "A law unto himself." He manages to play by his own rules even within a tough corporate structure. He'll rebel at an injustice wherever he sees it. He'll join the bowling team but avoid the annual picnic or vice versa.

You never know what will happen when your Aquarius office pal is around. That's why they're so much fun.

IF YOU ARE AN AQUARIUS

Be fair with others, but keep after them until they're fair with you.

ALAN ALDA (JANUARY 28)

You're the zodiac's champion of the underdog. Like Pisces, you have an idealist view of how things should be. The difference is that you never tire of trying new ways to put your dreams into action. You quickly become an expert at anything you learn, and you're always willing to share your ideas and your know-how.

How then can you push your career out of the no-zone into the ozone?

Put a Sock in It

You have great ideas most of the time. Your ability to look at an issue from an uncommon perspective makes you an invaluable employee. It's when your know-it-all gene kicks in and you can't stop yammering, even when your boss or coworkers don't want to hear it, that you get in trouble.

As a Fixed sign you automatically assume your way is the best way. As an Air sign, you're born with a politician's supply of hot air. This combination can be deadly to your career, especially since you also have little regard for where or when you launch into one of your verbal missives.

Trapping a VIP in the elevator will backfire when he shoves you out on the twentieth floor and you have to walk back down to your office. And trying to use a staff meeting to prove that the boss's money-savings plan is outdated can get you fired.

If you have a proposal for the boss, outline your idea and put it on her desk. If you want the attention of a power player, ask for a meeting. There's a time and place for everything. There's also a difference between taking advantage of a sudden opportunity and coming across as just another slob with a half-baked idea. Your ideas are usually great. Be professional about presenting them, and you can pull off a coup.

Don't Overanalyze

Mutable Air Gemini rationalizes. Mutable Earth Virgo justifies. Mutable Fire Sagittarius philosophizes. But your Fixed Air can get so carried away that you can spend hours trying to decide what the clerk at the local minimart really meant when he said, "Good morning."

Along with Uranus's genius for cutting through the crap to get to the bottom of an issue, you inherited his overactive imagination. You can be as paranoid as a Scorpio, only your suspicions border on worldwide conspiracy theories and plots to get you fired.

You worry yourself sick over whether or not the boss, a coworker, or the guy in the next cubicle is out to get you. When you're worried, you spend hours venting your fears to your coworkers, friends, or anyone who'll listen. The more you vent, the worse you feel. Why? You think you're analyzing the situation, but in reality you're feeding your paranoia.

Next time you think something's wrong, approach the person and ask. Go to your boss if you feel as if you're being left out of the loop on an issue that might affect your job. Nine times out of ten, a professional, direct approach will clear the air. And if it's the tenth time, chances are there's nothing you can do about it, so don't drive yourself nuts over something you can't change.

TIPS FOR SUCCESS

- Admit when you're wrong
- Quit bitching
- Learn to take advice

Know When to Complain

Everyone gets down now and then, or irked with the boss, or bored with work. Most people keep their worries to themselves or only vent them to close family and friends.

When you get in a snit, everything in your world looks bad, and being the Masculine Fixed Air sign that you are, every person in your world knows about it. You bitch about your rotten day to everyone from the bank teller and the cafeteria server to the crew at work. When you're in a snit, you're likely to fly off the handle at an issue as innocuous as a change of toilet paper in the company restroom.

You're the zodiac's crusader for fair play, but when you go off on everything from the air temperature to the green beans you had for lunch, you make yourself look bad. Plus you're in danger of not being taken seriously when you're truly upset about something serious.

Save your righteous anger for heavy issues such as unfair labor practices, on-the-job harassment, or outing a dishonest coworker. Otherwise you'll come across as just another crank with hostility issues.

FROM FED UP TO FIRED UP

I have lost almost three hundred games. I have failed over and over again . . . and that's precisely why I succeed.

MICHAEL JORDAN (FEBRUARY 17)

You never give up. Whether it's climbing to the top of your field or plowing through an overflowing in-box, you won't quit until you've finished your work. You usually learn from your mistakes, and you have a knack for seeing the finish line before you even have a plan of action. Your challenge is twofold: learn to recognize a brick wall when you hit it and admit that you need assistance sometimes just like everyone else.

Accept Help

One of your worst traits is trying to do everything yourself. Even when you ask for assistance, you want to control how and when it's given.

I knew a Water Bearer who was put in charge of the annual department picnic. She delegated tasks to her team of work buddies who had volunteered to help. Along with the task list, she handed out instructions on where to buy the decorations, what brands of food to get, the best color for the tablecloths, and on and on and on. She drove herself and everyone else crazy. Finally, when most of her helpers had told her to take a flying leap, she was forced to admit she couldn't do it alone and backed off.

You have a "if you want it done right, do it yourself" attitude. What you need to learn is that most of your colleagues are just as capable as you are. Most people want to do a good job, just as you do. Start small if you want to, but learn to trust your team or the person whose help you're taking. Otherwise, your control-freak ways will ensure that you get what you wish for—to do it yourself.

Know When to Quit

Aquarian inventor Thomas Edison said, "I've never worked a day in my life. It was all fun."

I had a close Aquarian friend who worked in a job she loved, even when her desk overflowed and the phones rang off the hook and a line of disgruntled customers were lined outside her door. Sometimes when I would call and asked what she was doing, she would reply, "Playing." It might sound loony to some, but that's how she felt about her work. To her it was a gift to be enjoyed, and she loved every minute, even when it was total chaos.

You need the freedom to pursue your ideas, whether that's helping your boss develop a new sales plan or working on a collective bargaining agreement with your coworkers. When your creativity and innovative spirit are stifled, you lose. You won't be happy every minute at any job, but ask yourself if your current job feels like fun, at least part of the time. If not, it might be time to go.

Ace an Interview

Your laid-back demeanor and ability to talk to anyone gets you off on the right foot. The way you shoot off your other foot is when you unleash your stream-of-consciousness ideas upon the unfortunate interviewer.

When the interviewer asks you why you're seeking a new position, you can go off about the right fit, the wrong fit, and vague references to meshing, clashing, and peaceful coexistence. While you're on your tangent, she's slipping into a coma. You need to practice the KISS (keep it simple, stupid) method of talking with a prospective employer. Stick to the facts.

Another way you can fumble the interview is by interrupting the person with questions of your own. You don't mean to be rude; your mind works so fast that if you don't spit it out when you think of it, it's gone.

Hint: Let it go. It's more important to look professional than to find out where she bought her earrings.

Some Aquarians have trouble concentrating when they're nervous. Their mind becomes so flooded with alternative answers that they come across as blathering bores. If you react like this, try focusing on the interviewer's voice. It can help to tune out your internal chatter. Once you do, your inner genius will appear. And when that happens, you'll ace every interview.

Aquarius-Friendly Careers

Humanitarian, volunteer organizer, activist, and electrical engineer are some of astrology's top jobs for you. You might not be a political rebel or fly around the world for a cause, but you probably regularly contribute either time or money to help better the world. What you need is a career that respects your nonconformist outlook and gives you the autonomy to pursue alternatives to the status quo.

Psychoanalyst

Your never-ending curiosity about what makes people tick, nonjudgmental attitude, and genuine concern for the welfare of every human you know makes you a natural at helping people solve their deepest problems.

Inventor

You have a far-sighted ability to see how to improve almost anything combined with a strong intuition of what will succeed. This blend gives you the edge in designing anything from a more efficient kitchen gadget to cutting-edge medical technology.

Pilot

Flying appeals to your desire to kick off the bonds of restraint. Plus you're fascinated by the mechanics that allow a megaton piece of metal to soar through the sky.

Alternative-Medicine Practitioner

Whether you're an herbalist or practice acupuncture or Reiki therapy, anything that's natural and nontraditional appeals to you.

Private Investigator

Digging up dirt on a wayward spouse or racing against time to rescue a missing person satisfies your need to see justice done.

CHAPTER THIRTEEN

Pisces
February 19–March 20

Element:	Water
Quality:	Mutable
Symbol:	The Fishes
Ruler:	Neptune
Key word:	Imaginative
Work-a-tude:	I don't need any help.

INSTANT INSIGHTS

I do take my work seriously. The way to do that is not to take yourself too seriously.

ALAN RICKMAN (FEBRUARY 21)

Pisces is Feminine Mutable Water. Astrology teaches us that a Fish contains traits of each of the signs preceding him, plus his own intuitive take on the people and events in his world. Pisces is ruled by Neptune, the planet of creativity, illusion, and self-delusion. Words associated with these natives are visionary, intuitive, and empathetic. The flip side of the Fish's tail is that he can get so lost in fantasizing about the ideal career or life that he never attempts to move outside the illusion to actually pursue his dream.

Adding to the confusion is Pisces's pad on the zodiac wheel. She lives in the Twelfth House of secrets, seclusion, and the occult. Here the word occult means things hidden from others or the self. The subconscious hangs out here. So does insight and the ability to see beneath the surface. Not every Pisces is a psychic, but they all are very perceptive about human nature. Male or female, a Pisces is often the colleague whom everyone else confides in, including the boss. His empathetic, nonjudgmental approach attracts people in the throes of either a personal or professional crisis. Because of his Twelfth House character, the Fish has an uncanny ability to unravel the motives behind a rival's actions.

Ever see a fish swimming in a clear lake? It might circle lazily around a log or lie quiet in a shallow pool. Let your shadow fall on it, and it darts away too fast for your eyes to follow. Emotionally, the human version of this final sign of the zodiac reacts the same way. Although these colleagues are good in a crisis and make committed team players, they try to avoid conflict with as much dedication as a Leo tries to avoid sharing the spotlight.

When it comes to helping coworkers, friends, or even strangers, he sees everyone else's life with crystal-clear reality. However, when it comes to himself, his clarity often gets fogged over by Neptune's emotional smoke-and-mirrors deception.

Mutable Air Gemini circulates ideas. Mutable Earth Virgo distributes criticisms. Mutable Fire Sagittarius hands out advice. Mutable Water Pisces, however, peers under the surface to see what's really going on: Secret enemies. Secret motives. Secret dreams.

PISCES ON THE JOB

Any activity becomes creative when the doer cares about doing it right, or better.

JOHN UPDIKE (MARCH 18)

Working with a Fish is similar to observing a magic act. Now you see him, now you don't. One day, your Pisces coworker will be in the middle of the latest crisis, providing insight, encouragement, and working overtime to help control the damage. The next, he'll disappear into his office or behind his desk and not speak to anyone. That's the way this dual-natured sign stays balanced.

FAMOUS VISIONARY FISH

- George Washington, first president of the United States (February 22)
- Ron Howard, Oscar-winning filmmaker (March 1)
- Albert Einstein, scientist/mathematician (March 14)

While the Twins of Gemini stand side by side, doubling this sign's need to constantly process information and sample new ideas, Pisces's Fishes swim in opposite directions. A common misconception is that one fish strives for success and the other plunges toward failure. This isn't true. The Fishes move between reality and the ideal. Your Pisces office mate understands the real world, he just doesn't always like living in it.

A Pisces work chum is open-minded, unbiased, and adaptable. She won't panic under pressure, and her outside-the-box thinking can result in an ingenious solution to a difficult situation. This coworker is fair, friendly, and always willing to share the load. Win her friendship by treating her the same way.

Managing a Fish
Provide Alternatives

Flexible Pisces can work with anyone and almost anywhere. She can handle complex issues independently or, like Libra, soothe a surly client. She'll calm a nervous applicant waiting for his interview and can entertain a two-year-old while his mom is in a dressing room.

She also has the need to withdraw now and then. If she works with the public, a rotating schedule that alternates between being in a hot spot and working behind the scenes can help get the optimal performance from her. Let her switch between the daily-meetings grind to working behind the scenes.

Wherever he is, a Pisces works best under steady pressure to perform. When he's busy, he'll work. When things are slow, he'll stretch a five-minute task into an hour. The same on-or-off attitude that makes him need solitude controls his self-motivation. Some slow days, he'll search for other work. Other days, he'll daydream the afternoon away while shuffling the same stack of papers around his desk.

Apply firm but fair guidelines and make her accountable, and you'll discover an efficient, high-producing employee who keeps her eyes on the bottom line and her ears to the underground.

Keep Them Enthused

The flexible Fish works well in a variety of situations. He's equally capable being in a group that's hammering out a new strategy or working independently in a quiet corner. Although he likes people, when working with the public, he prefers one-on-one situations such as interviewing job applicants or meeting vendors by appointment. Let him teach orientation classes or take newbies on a tour of the company. Make him deal with crowds rushing a busy store counter or reception desk, and the Fish will dive for cover.

If you want to assess the mood of your boss, a client, or a roomful of VIPs at a monthly marketing meeting, park your Pisces in close proximity. It will take about a minute for him to know whether you can relax or should keep your guard up.

She doesn't like surprises and can freeze at being thrown into an unfamiliar situation. The more lead time you can give of an impending change, the better chance you'll have of avoiding a meltdown. Once she's had time to absorb the idea, she'll handle it with professionalism and style.

One of the easiest ways to motivate a Pisces is with a simple thank-you. A Fish needs reassurance, and showing him that you appreciate what he does will make him even more determined to do a great job.

Beware of the Space Cadet

The Fish's head is screwed firmly on her shoulders, but sometimes no one, including her, knows in which direction it's pointed. Pisces can tackle a multipart project with the efficiency of an Aquarius examining a tax report, then forget it's her turn to watch the phones.

Dropping a huge task on his desk can overwhelm some Fish. If that happens, he might take a trip to Procrastination Land either out of fear that he won't be able to handle it or by deluding himself that he can wait to the last minute and bang it out. Assign periodic deadlines. Check in frequently with encouragement, and he'll relax. You can, too. Despite his spacey rep, when a Fish dedicates himself to doing a good job, he rarely fails.

Pisces swims in two worlds—reality and imagination. In world one, she's grounded, organized, and clever. In world two, she's vague, unpredictable, and either emotionally or physically MIA.

Your job is to help keep her grounded in reality without stifling her inspiration and insight. Provide reality checks by asking her input on a project. Assign a task that utilizes her organizational skills. Then let her sit in on a planning session to redesign the workflow or help plan a fundraiser. When you help your Fish link her dual worlds, she'll help you turn yours into a productive, smoothly running one.

Surviving Boss Fish
Know What You're Dealing With

It's a rare Fish who wants to swim all the way to the CEO's office. They certainly exist. Think ex-Disney boss Michael Eisner. Although working for Disney Enterprises was probably a fantasy-fulfilling job for a Fish, the point is that he's the ex-boss. Few Fish stick out a whole career in the corporate world. As of this writing, Eisner's hosting his own TV talk show interviewing high-powered people from all walks of life—creative, fun, and one-on-one.

Because he's sensitive to your needs, you can get away with a few late mornings and long lunches. However, don't get lulled into a false sense of security. Boss Fish can go from goldfish to tiger shark in an instant. Fortunately, the outburst is over just as quickly.

Whether your Boss Fish is in the glass-walled office on the top floor or inventing cocktails at his own corner bar, he often flip-flops between sticking to policy and ignoring the rules. His inconsistency is frustrating, but his motives are well meant. Boss Fish includes the human factor in deciding what's best for the business, and that doesn't always mesh with the policy manual. He's also full of creative ideas but has a hard time channeling them into conventional paths. Pitch in to help him make his plans work, and you'll earn a permanent spot on this boss's staff.

Be Alert

Although he can handle the day-to-day craziness of a busy season or a last-minute crunch as well as any other boss, a couple of things can happen to the Fish when the pressure's on. He'll either become absentminded and easily distracted, or he'll get as testy as a Capricorn who's just lost a megamoney deal. Both if the crisis is critical.

Either way, you need to keep your cool. All Pisces work best when they can talk through a dilemma. That's why this boss is surprisingly open to hearing your opinions. She'll appreciate it if you offer her the same compassionate ear as she does you. Giving her a chance to vent in private can help her to keep from unleashing her angst at the staff in general. Plus she'll usually discover a solution during the process.

Like Aries, Leo, and Gemini, this boss only handles details when he's forced to. Stay on top of his daily activities and keep him on track with frequent reminders. Along with Sagittarius, the Fish isn't likely to sit in his office all day, so encourage him to carry a cell phone so you can reach him at all times. Knowing that he has your ear and that you have his back cements your relationship with this kindhearted boss.

PISCES WORDS TO LIVE BY

"You can't undo the past, but you can certainly not repeat it."
—Bruce Willis (March 19)

"You have to be able to make decisions on your own."
—Rupert Murdoch (March 11)

Use Your Imagination

When working for a Pisces, sooner or later you're bound to catch him staring out the window, lost in thought. It might look as if he's slacking off, but when this boss lets his mind wander, he comes up with some of his most brilliant ideas.

While I don't recommend that you drop everything to stare out the window, too, the Fish is one boss who won't automatically dismiss your creative ideas. He won't steal them, either. What he will do is listen with interest. If he thinks your suggestion will work, he'll help you to develop it and see that it gets presented at the next management meeting. Some bosses see a savvy employee as a potential rival, but Boss Fish feels that it only proves that he's the savvy one for hiring you.

Keeping this boss on track by being superorganized will win his approval and appreciation. But if you can keep a steady supply of creative ideas flowing in his direction, he'll think you're a genius and that he can't do without you.

Coping with a Pisces Coworker

Like Aquarius, a Fish is concerned with helping others succeed. The difference is that while the Water Bearer's visions are often large scale, aimed at the collective workforce or the world, the Fish takes the personal approach. He'll loan you lunch money, listen to your problems, and warn you when to keep your head down. He'll also keep you entertained with his outrageous humor, and his camaraderie can help to keep morale high during a crisis.

Never Underestimate Them

Astrology books often refer to Pisces as the egoless sign. The common translation is that Pisces is the doormat of the zodiac. This isn't exactly true. It is true that your Pisces workmate has a hard time turning down a request for assistance and would rather step back than rush into a confrontation. This might make you think you can get away with anything. Wrong.

I once knew a Fish who finally had it with a pushy coworker who constantly bombarded her for help, then was conveniently too busy to reciprocate when the Pisces was on overload. From that day until the other person left about six months later, the Fish managed to avoid her at every turn. Invitations to lunch were politely refused. The constant requests for help were turned down, but always in a professional manner. When she's had enough, your average Pisces simply turns off. She doesn't have time to waste on people she doesn't like. Fortunately, it takes a lot to turn your Fishy friend into a human iceberg.

If a Pisces likes you, he'll do anything for you, including midnight rides to the hospital or 2:00 a.m. rescues when you're too drunk to drive. Earn his friendship by not taking advantage of his accommodating nature, and you'll earn yourself a friend for life.

Keep Your Guard Up

Bad Fish are rarely after your job. He might daydream about being boss or running the company, but in reality, he likes being just another anonymous face in the crowd.

Where you run into trouble with this coworker is when his paranoia gets out of hand and he thinks he's been overlooked, slighted, or backstabbed. Then you have a Fish that will bite you at every turn. Pisces anger is the passive-aggressive kind. She might "forget" to tell you the boss called an emergency meeting or ask him if you can help her with a project instead of going directly to you. She'll be nice to your face, then talk about you behind your back. If you confront her, she'll deny everything and probably convince you of her innocence. As soon as you walk away, her underground feud will start again.

Ignore her gossiping. If she's talking about you, you can bet this puny Fish is talking about everyone. Handle her backstabbing with an out-in-the-open offer of help, such as at break or lunch time. Make sure she's within earshot when you casually tell the boss that she apologized for making you late to the meeting. Nothing stops a bottom-feeding Fish faster than making her confront her bad behavior.

PISCES CHEAP SHOTS

- Leaves you out of the information loop
- Goes to the boss instead of asking you directly for help
- Takes days off when you're overloaded

Learn to Love Them

It's hard not to like a Pisces. They are accommodating, social, and funny. This coworker keeps to herself, won't spill a secret, and is always ready to give you a pep talk should you get down.

As a Water sign, the Fish takes every criticism personally, no matter how well meant. The difference is that instead of biting back as the Crab does, a Fish emotionally flees the scene. This doesn't mean you have to treat your Pisces with kid gloves, but it helps if you always approach him in a nonthreatening manner. Try not to bark at him, but don't patronize, either—he's a champ at reading between the lines.

Yes, she'll space out now and then. Yes, she might flake on a girls' night out. But when you need advice, a shoulder to lean on, or assistance with a time-consuming task, you can always count on a Pisces.

IF YOU ARE A PISCES

Don't let other people tell you what you want.

PAT RILEY (MARCH 20)

Pisces Albert Einstein said, "Imagination is more important than knowledge." In your case, *imagination* and *intuition* are nearly synonymous. You instinctively know what will please your boss, soothe a frazzled coworker, or calm an angry customer. This makes you the go-to person for metaphorical tea and sympathy. However, when you're envisioning the next fashion fad or movie trend, you're also tapping into your psychic intuition and blending the two into creative genius.

So how can you make a permanent transition from professional babysitter to powerful trendsetter?

Stay in the Moment

While Virgo strives for order in its world, you're the sign that craves the idealistic sense of perfection: Ideal world. Ideal relationship. Ideal job.

Here's how you set yourself up to fail: Your Neptune-ruled tendency to fantasize either a best- or worst-case scenario can cripple your career. Thinking the worst can make you give up before you try. Conversely, you could get so caught up in writing your Oscar acceptance speech before you write the screenplay that you never start the work. Procrastination created from self-delusion is your Achilles' heel.

All too often, you decide to throw in the towel about two seconds too soon. You hear a cutback's coming or you know that the boss is unhappy, and you automatically assume that yours will be the first head to roll. So you quit rather than risk the humiliation of being laid off. Instead of letting fear run away with your common sense, step back from the issue. Stick to the facts. Think about your options. If you're behind on a project, tell the boss before you miss the deadline. If you're worried about a rumor, don't panic—discuss it. Hiding your head in the sand only makes you look bad and can whip your already overactive anxiety gene into a panicked frenzy.

All Water signs hate confrontation, but you imagine conflict where none is intended.

TIPS FOR SUCCESS

- Follow your dream, not someone else's
- Trust your intuition
- Stay focused

Trust Your Gut

Your strongest trait is the instinct to instantly peg a person's intentions. You have near-perfect internal radar that can either reassure you or warn you to be cautious. It also can guide you to make uncannily accurate assessments when you should make a career move.

The trouble starts when you second-guess yourself. Scorpio might rarely give anyone the benefit of the doubt, but you go overboard in the other direction. You can listen to everyone *but* yourself. In trying to be fair, or trying to avoid conflict, you let others take the lead and can end up regretting it. When you're on the wrong track, your inner voice never stops nagging, but you have to train yourself to listen to it instead of letting others' opinions cloud your judgment.

One way to do this is to turn your Eager-to-Please-o-Stat down to simmer. Listen to the advice, suggestion, or idea, then give yourself at least twenty-four hours to think it over. Nine times out of ten, when you cool your jets and think about it, you'll do the right thing for yourself.

Quit Hoping and Start Intending

Similar to Virgo and Taurus, you get stuck in a rut. However, your issue is that you often ignore facts staring you in the face in favor of "hoping" things will miraculously get resolved. You "wish" for a break.

When you leave your career up to fate or to the whims of others, you allow Neptune's escapism to rule. You're deceiving yourself and, worse, avoiding taking the responsibility for steering your career.

Scorpions are desert dwellers that can live on little moisture. Crabs are both land and sea creatures. You're a water-dwelling Fish, however, and water takes the path of least resistance. Your natural proclivities are to drift along until something shakes your world, then to duck your head and *hope* you survive.

Practice this. Each time you think or say either hope or wish, correct it to intend. Instead of, "I *hope* I get this job," say, "I *intend* to do my best to get this job." Instead of, "I *wish* I'd get a lucky break," say, "I *intend* to make my own luck. What can I do to give myself a better chance?"

This is good advice for all of us. However, it's crucial for you. Apply this simple rule to every aspect of your life, and you'll be amazed at how fast you can go from sitting in the back row feeling neglected to standing in the spotlight giving that acceptance speech.

FROM FED UP TO FIRED UP

You're really got to start hitting the books, because it's no joke out here.

SPIKE LEE (MARCH 20)

Wise, funny, and quick to make friends, you bring a sense of calmness to the workplace. You often become the unofficial therapist for your colleagues and can have the toughest boss eating out of your hand. Your challenge is to learn the difference between being flexible and helpful and neglecting your own needs.

Stand Up for Yourself

Like Gemini and Sagittarius, you have a hard time saying no. Gemini gets overloaded because she doesn't want to miss anything, and Sagittarius gets overwhelmed because he thinks he can solve every problem. In your case, you put yourself last on the list of people to help.

Although you love being the one everyone comes to, your penchant for putting their wants ahead of yours is a sure way to kill your career. It might be a heady trip thinking that you are all things to all people, but it's also self-delusional. Not to mention, dumb. Unless you value your time, few others will.

If you want to get ahead, you must learn to recognize when you're being taking advantage of. You also need to understand that assertive and aggressive are not synonymous terms. Take an assertiveness training class. You already know how to handle the rest of the world. Once you can handle yourself, you'll own it.

Know When to Quit

As much as you might hate your work or dislike your boss, you often stick with a sure thing instead of finding something new.

Pushing out of your comfort zone is as uncomfortable to you as it is for any Fixed sign. The difference is that you have a built-in guilt complex the size of Neptune that also traps you. *You can't leave your office buddies in the lurch. Your boss really isn't that bad. At least you have a job.* Although your compassion is admirable, it won't pay the rent after you've been fired because your frustration with a job you hate has caused you to screw it up. Facing facts isn't one of your strong points, Fish. But if you want to get ahead in life, and save your sanity in the meantime, that's what you must do.

The five signs of burnout are apathy, irritability, clock watching, increased sick time, and passing up happy hour. If you have more than one of these at a time, or any of them all the time, then it's time to go.

Once you start the job search, you'll get excited. Your friends will root for you, and you might inspire them to make their moves, too. You deserve the best, Fishy. Don't let fear or a misplaced sense of loyalty hold you back.

Ace an Interview

Your professional look and quiet confidence gets you escorted in the door, and your knack for putting other people at ease helps set the stage for a relaxed conversation. If *you* could only relax, you'd save yourself from being shuffled out again in record time.

You can try so hard to please that you lose yourself in the process. Instead of being yourself, you flub the interview by trying to anticipate what the person wants to hear. Here's a hint: No one wants a clone. Answer the questions as you see them. You didn't get this far by being stupid.

As do Gemini, Sagittarius, and Virgo, you can babble useless facts without taking a breath. Plus your mind can go completely blank, and you can't think of a word to say. When you blather, the interviewer thinks you're just another brainless twit. When you freeze, you make the person you're talking with so uncomfortable that he clams up, too.

Try this. You have a good imagination. Look at the guy sitting across from you as just another working slob doing his job. Once you see him as a human being and not some scary authority figure, you'll relax. When you relax, you connect. And when you connect, you win.

Pisces-Friendly Careers

Astrology teaches that you're mystical, inspired, and artistic. Of course, this doesn't mean that you'll automatically want to be either a holistic healer or a portrait painter, although you could probably do either very well. What it means is that whether you're a lawyer, a doctor, or a business owner, you need a career that allows you to express your unique ideas and vision.

The following are a few that you might find inspiring.

Theater Arts

Whether you're directing a play, starring in it, designing the costumes, or writing the script, helping to create a world of illusion and unleashing your vivid fantasies can make you rich.

Advertising Executive

Your knack for knowing how to glamorize an everyday item and envision the next big fad ensures you a well-paid career telling the public what they need.

Marine Scientist

Working to save the oceans you love, as well as the life within them, meshes with your idealism to make the world a more perfect place. Bonus: You get to live at the beach.

Musician

Whether as a singer, songwriter, concert pianist, or rocker keyboardist, you could create original, imaginative melodies that could make you a star.

Life Coach

No one's better than you at giving unconditional support and intuitive advice to people who need a boost of confidence to help them succeed.

Acknowledgments

My grateful thanks to the following workmates for their support and friendship: Mary Norris, my diplomatic and thoughtful Libra editor; Sagittarians Marta De La Torre and Mike Baldwin; Scorpio Debbie Chappell; Leo Anne Perez; and Aries Betty Wineland.

About the Author

Hazel Dixon-Cooper is *Cosmopolitan* magazine's Cosmo Astrologer and the author of the internationally best-selling humorous astrology books *Born on a Rotten Day, Love on a Rotten Day,* and *Friends on a Rotten Day.*

She is a professional astrologer, teacher of astrology, and a research member of the American Federation of Astrologers. She lives in California.